I0437133

Pressure Cooker

Author's Note

This is the latest edition of Pressure Cooker: An Immigrant's Journey. The first edition was published by Author House in 2015 and the second by LitPrime Solutions in August 2023. I had signed a contract with LitPrime for rebranding and marketing of this book in July of 2023, but terminated it in November of 2023, for cause. LitPrime has gone underground since the termination of our contract and has not returned the manuscript, two screenplays, and a query letter which a LitPrime official claimed were needed for the marketing of my book. On January 18, 2024, I sent a letter by Certified Mail to Amazon KDP to request the immediate unpublishing of the edition by LitPrime Solutions. LitPrime's actions have necessitated the publishing of this latest edition with a new cover and pictures depicting some of the major scenes and events. The expectation is to make this book available on all the platforms at Amazon-KDP, Barnes & Noble, e-books, foreign languages, audiobooks, etc.

Koff Mensane
February 2024

Pressure Cooker

An Immigrant's Journey

KOFF MENSANE

authorHOUSE®

AuthorHouse™
1663 Liberty Drive
Bloomington, IN 47403
www.authorhouse.com
Phone: 833-262-8899

© 2012 Koff Mensane. All rights reserved.

No part of this book may be reproduced, stored in
a retrieval system, or transmitted by any means
without the written permission of the author.

Published by AuthorHouse   06/06/2024

ISBN: 978-1-4772-9647-9 (sc)
ISBN: 978-1-4772-9648-6 (e)

Library of Congress Control Number: 2012923122

Print information available on the last page.

Any people depicted in stock imagery provided by Getty Images are
models, and such images are being used for illustrative purposes only.
Certain stock imagery © Getty Images.

This book is printed on acid-free paper.

Because of the dynamic nature of the Internet, any web
addresses or links contained in this book may have changed
since publication and may no longer be valid. The views
expressed in this work are solely those of the author and do
not necessarily reflect the views of the publisher, and the
publisher hereby disclaims any responsibility for them.

Contents

CHAPTER 1

Home Country

In September 1967, Ifok was admitted to the local university to study for a certificate in community development. He had originally applied to study for a bachelor's degree in public administration, but had settled for the community development program after he failed to obtain high grades in all the subjects required for admission to study for the degree in public administration.

After his graduation in June 1970, Ifok was hired by the government as a development assistant on a salary of $2,000 per annum. He was stationed at the regional office of the Department of Community Development in the capital city of the country. This department was responsible for approving all applications for development.

Ifok liked his new job. He was born in the capital city and had spent most of his life there, and his parents lived and owned property there. His parents offered him a rent-free flat in their three-storey home. A few months after he started working at the regional office, Ifok, like most of the professional staff of this department, started taking jobs on the side. He prepared plans for developers and submitted them to his department for approval. These jobs brought him almost as much as he was being paid by the government. Being single and without dependants, he spent a substantial part of his money entertaining friends, mainly women. He went to night clubs about thrice a week and stayed out till about 2:00 AM. He, however, managed to be in his office by 8:30 in the morning each work day. The government also gave him a loan to purchase a personal car, thereby giving him wings to fly.

Ifok's parents did not approve of the kind of life he was living. His mother was especially resentful of his promiscuous activities, because Ifok's father had a reputation as a womanizer during his younger days and she did not want any of her children to follow that path. She used to tell Ifok that women were not like food for a man to change his menu every day. If she answered the phone and it was a woman asking to speak with Ifok, she would often tell her Ifok had gone out without bothering to find out if he was home or not. Ifok's parents decided to have a conference with him about his lifestyle. This conference took place early one Saturday morning.

INTERVENTION BY PARENTS

"We have summoned you here to talk about your lifestyle," started Kobi, Ifok's father. "Your mother and I believe that you are living a promiscuous lifestyle, and that you do not respect us," he continued.

"Oh! You know I respect you. What have I done wrong?" Ifok asked.

"We have been seeing you bring different women to your flat. What are you trying to achieve by doing all that?" Ifok's mother, Adeye, asked.

"Mother, they are my friends," Ifok said.

"If that is the case, then you have too many female friends," Adeye said. "A man is supposed to have a few female friends he will meet in public places, and a special one he should get to know well, marry and establish a family with," she continued.

"Okay" Ifok said.

"Let us know the woman you would like to marry and we will bear all the expenses for your engagement to her," Kobi said.

"Also, how much money have you saved since you started working?" Adeye asked.

"About $50" Ifok responded.

"My God, you mean you have worked for a year and you have only $50 in the bank? Kobi, our son is messing up his life," Adeye said.

"From now on, you should save, at least $20 a month and show your bank book to your mother anytime you do so. We are going to have a lot of problems if you do not do that," Kobi ordered.

"Yes, Dad" Ifok said.

Ifok decided to follow his parents' advice and make positive changes in his life; he minimized his partying, and saved as much of his income as possible. Within six months he became engaged to his favorite girlfriend, Gama, with the intention of marrying her as soon as she became pregnant. In the society in which he lived, marriage was mainly for procreation, and it was unusual to find a young couple childless after two years of marriage. Gama became pregnant a month after their engagement and they were married in a civil ceremony a month before she gave birth to a boy. The child was named Rojo.

In January 1973, the government as part of its decentralization plan opened district development offices throughout the country to be headed by development assistants. Ifok was appointed to head the district office in Edumaf, a village just 50 miles away but without electricity, and devoid of all the attractions of the big city. He decided that his wife and son would stay in the city, mainly because of its medical facilities, and that he would be back every weekend to be with them.

Edumaf, a small village on the coast of the Atlantic Ocean had a population of 3,000 in 1973. Eighty percent of the people were fishermen, twelve percent were engaged in farming and trading, and the remaining eight percent were involved in local administration and other occupations. Only ten persons who lived in the village owned cars, and Ifok happened to be one of them. It was not surprising, therefore, that most of the young women liked him, and most of the young men did not. For someone used to the bright lights of the big city, life in Edumaf was very depressing, especially at night. The main street was usually deserted by 6:00 PM, and apart from a few food sellers and two bars, there was no night life. Ifok compensated for this lack of nocturnal activities by drinking more and sleeping with any woman who made herself available. Within six months he had four women as his regular lovers. Such a promiscuous life, especially in a small town like Edumaf, was likely to land anyone in trouble. Ifok could just not avoid trouble.

One Wednesday evening in December, 1973, one of Ifok's regular lovers, Maa, decided to stay for the night rather than go home after spending time with Ifok. Her explanation was that her folks had gone out of town and that she was afraid to be alone in the house at night. Actually, Maa had lied just to be in Ifok's company longer; her parents had not gone out of town and were looking for her.

Nuger, a farmer who lived in Ifok's building and was a close friend of Maa's relatives, had seen her entering Ifok's apartment but did not know her parents were looking for her. He was drinking with Paatiko, Maa's uncle, at the local bar when Paatiko told him his niece had not been home in two days. Nuger immediately informed him that he had seen Maa entering Ifok's apartment two days ago. On hearing this, Paatiko ordered a pint of local gin, shared it with Nuger and the two of them rushed to Maa's house to give her folks the good news.

A meeting of the family was immediately summoned at which Nuger narrated where and when he had seen Maa. A delegation made up of the young woman's uncles was appointed to go to Ifok's house to check out Nuger's story. Maa's grandmother, Alaba, decided to accompany the delegation because she wanted to have "a little chat" with the man who had "abducted" her granddaughter.

This delegation arrived at Ifok's house about 9:00 PM. By then Ifok and Maa were in bed listening to rock music. Paatiko pounded on the door and when Ifok asked who it was, he lied stating that he was a fisherman who wanted Ifok to prepare some building plans for him. Thinking he was going to make an extra buck, Ifok quickly opened the door, only to be confronted by four heavily muscled men and a gray-haired old woman who immediately slapped Ifok while asking the question: "The woman you are with, is she your wife?" The men rushed to the bedroom and grabbed Maa before she could jump out of a window. Before she left Ifok's house, Alaba slapped Ifok two more times and told him he would be hearing from her family within the next few days. Since it was Friday and Ifok had to go to his wife and son in the big city the next day anyway, he decided to leave right way in order to avoid further attacks that night.

Ifok was not his usual self that weekend and was very quiet most of the time. After all, he was carrying a heavy burden. His wife noticed the change in his attitude.

"You are exceptionally quiet and are not eating much. What is the problem?" Gama asked.

"I am not feeling too well. I guess I am getting tired of spending five days of every week in a rural area while my family remains in the city," he responded.

"Don't worry, Rojo and I will come and stay with you at Edumaf in a year's time, she said.

"Okay" Ifok said.

As one would expect, his thoughts were actually on events likely to occur on his return to work on Monday. He thought Maa's relatives would come to his office and create a scene, thereby embarrassing him in the presence of his staff. He never expected them to file a police report since he never kept Maa against her will. Maa was a consenting adult.

To Ifok's surprise, Maa's relatives filed a compliant at the local police station accusing him of abduction and having sexual relations with a young woman who was not his wife. They told the police that Maa was 17 years old. How could she be 17 when she graduated from high school two years ago? Well, in Edumaf at that time, not everyone had a birth certificate and a statement by a parent was sometimes considered adequate proof of age. This was considered one of those times.

Ifok heard of the charges filed against him as soon as he arrived at his office on Monday morning.

"Good morning, how are you?" Ifok asked, his administrative assistant.

"Good morning, Sir. I am fine and I hope you are also okay," Tobi responded.

"I do not know about being okay," Ifok said.

"I have this message for you. Inspector Crabbo wants you to report at the police station as soon as possible," Tobi said, with a concerned expression on his face.

"Thank you very much," Ifok said, walking out the door to go to the police station. "If anyone comes looking for me let him wait. I will be right back," Ifok concluded.

At the police station, Ifok was allowed to post a $20 bond, pending an appearance in court in three weeks. Inspector Crabbo advised Ifok to get in touch with Maa's relatives and settle the issue out of court. To do this, Ifok had to get some prominent members of the community to talk to this family on his behalf. He selected Mank, a retired surveyor, and Akoko, a retired civil servant as his representatives. They contacted Maa's family and a date was set for a meeting to settle the issue. Ifok was to provide the refreshments for this meeting.

Three days before this scheduled meeting, around 8.00 PM, Ifok was at home relaxing and listening to the radio when he heard a soft knock on the door. Ifok answered, "Who is it?" and the person knocking stated, "I am Lakotse, your friend."

"I do not know who you are. I do not have a friend by that name," Ifok stated. The person at the door continued knocking and asking Ifok to open the door. When Ifok opened the door, he recognized the face of the person who had come to his house. He was a frail old man who walked with a cane and lived nearby. He had always exchanged greetings and pleasantries with Ifok whenever they had met but Ifok did not know his name. Ifok's past interaction with him had never gone beyond basic friendly exchanges. He seemed to like Ifok.

Ifok invited him to come in but Lakotse did not, and rather suggested they should go and sit on a bench conveniently situated at the entrance of Ifok's compound. "I am here as a friend, to help you as necessary to deal with the problem you are having," he stated, obviously referring to the issue involving the young woman. "Thank you very much. I need all the help I can get," Ifok replied.

"You are having this problem because of tribalism and hostility toward foreigners. Anyone born and raised elsewhere is considered a foreigner at this place. This is common in other parts of this country too. You were born and raised in the capital city, a more cosmopolitan setting, so I do not think you understand how people in rural areas think and act. My friend, my son, the woman you had the affair with is 20 years old, and the marriageable age in this town is 16; additionally, polygamy is allowed here and you can have more than one wife. Despite these facts, these people will try to make money off of this non-issue or mess up your career in the civil service." Lakotse continued.

What Lakotse just said gave Ifok a better understanding of what was going on. It was his lifestyle and the fact that he was not a native of the area which had antagonized some people against him.

"There is a planned meeting to resolve this issue, and I will do my best to bring it to an end," Ifok said.

"Good. Solve this problem fast. Let me know if I can be of help," Lakotse concluded. With those parting words, Lakotse left for his house and Ifok never saw him again since he died a day later in his sleep. The encounter with Lakotse prepared Ifok well for his meeting with Maa's relatives.

Paafordee, the head of Maa's family made the opening statement at this meeting, and that indicated to Ifok that he was in for a tough fight.

"We have gathered here this evening to settle a very serious issue involving one of our daughters and this man (pointing to Ifok), the district officer," he started. "He abducted our daughter and repeatedly made love to her for two days. Under our laws that is another way of declaring intention to marry. I am, therefore, suggesting that he should perform the necessary rites and marry our daughter," he said.

"I can not marry her," Ifok said.

"Why?" asked Paafordee.

"I can not marry her because I am already married," Ifok said.

"I see. You are from the big city, and you are copying the white man's ways blindly. You marry one woman but then keep concubines on the side. We, village people, have more sense than you people and marry as many women as we can support," Paafordee said. Maa's relatives present, mostly men applauded, and Ifok realized that even Akoko and Mank were nodding. The women, on the other hand, just sat there silently, probably because they themselves were married to men with many wives.

"We are going to teach you a lesson which you will never forget as long as you live," Paafordee continued. "We are not going to tolerate your decadent lifestyle in this village. Our decision is this: You either marry our daughter or pay $200," Paafordee said.

"Oh no! That is too much money. There have been similar situations in this village and the offenders were not asked to pay one-tenth of that amount," Mank said.

"Yes, but those cases involved local residents with firm roots here," Paafordeee said. "But this man, a foreigner, just came here and started sleeping with all these women. He deserves a heavy punishment so that next time he sees a young, beautiful woman he will think twice before allowing his penis to do the talking," he continued. Everybody laughed.

"Okay, we will pay $120," Akoko pleaded

"We will settle for $150. Of this amount, $50 will be given to Maa, another $50 will be given to her family, and the remainder will be used to perform the traditional ceremony to make Maa a marriageable woman again." Paafordee said.

Before Akoko or Mank could ask for further reductions, Ifok got up and said: "I will pay the $150." He was happy the ordeal was over. His wife and parents did not know about this case and he wanted it to remain that way. He effected payment of this sum in a week.

It was after this ordeal that Ifok seriously started considering leaving for the United States. He felt that if he had passed all his examinations and gone on to study Public Administration he would have had a permanent job in the capital city and would never have been transferred to a village like Edumaf with no electricity. He felt that if he went to the United States and studied up to graduate level, he could come back to his country and get a nice job in the city. After all, the course he had taken was geared to rural, and not, urban development. He also felt that if he managed to stay in the United States for, at least, five years after completing his education he would be able to come home with enough money to lay the foundation for his "Empire." With his parents' promise to bear his educational expenses in the United States, he drew up a nine-year development plan made up of the following:1st Year—saving money for airfare to the United States and other expenses; 2nd to 4th Year—further studies in the United States, with his wife joining him within a year; 5th to 8th Year—working and saving money; and 9th Year—preparation for trip back home. The remainder of this story deals with Ifok's attempts to implement his plan.

CHAPTER 2

Early Stage Of Plan

There were two ways by which Ifok could come by enough money for his airfare to the United States: through saving a substantial part of his meager income, and obtaining more jobs on the side.

Saving a substantial part of his income was almost impossible since he had a car note in addition to supporting his wife and son. Unable to save money for two months, Ifok realized his best chance for saving any funds laid in the other option, namely, the preparation of plans for private developers. Fortunately for him, the potential for making money through this route was great in Edumaf, where only about twenty percent of the owners of buildings had obtained building permits; the remaining eighty percent had built their houses without submitting any plans to the Department of Community Development for approval.

Ifok sent out letters to all property owners in Edumaf requesting that they report at his office within a month with the permits that authorized them to build their houses. He also sought and obtained the support of the local chief and the Town Development Committee, and the permit inspection drive was announced at all local functions and activities. Those with the right permits had copies made and kept in the district office as required by law. Those who did not have permits mostly came to the office and sought Ifok's advice on how to obtain them. Ifok explained to them that any licensed draughtsman could prepare such plans. Since there were no draughtsmen in Edumaf, most of these people sought Ifok's help in having such plans completed. Ifok usually offered to prepare plans for existing buildings for a fee of $80 a building; this was $20 less than the fee usually charged by licensed draughtsmen. He undertook these projects with his two technical assistants, and usually paid them fifty percent of the price charged. Within two months they had about twenty jobs worth $1,600, out of which Ifok got about $800. This was more than enough to cover his airfare to the United States.

Ifok's initial application for a student visa was denied because he inadvertently told the consular officer that he planned to work part-time, if necessary, to supplement money promised by his parents.

"You will have to provide proof of sufficient funds for the duration of your stay. There are unemployed persons in the United States and jobs are not easy to come by," the consular officer told Ifok. Ifok's parents did not have a lump sum readily available for his expenses; they had property, the yearly income from which was more than enough to cover his expenses in the United States. Additionally, his father received yearly commissions of more than $5,000 abroad and he had these paid in to his bank accounts in London and New York. His father had one of the American companies he dealt with swear an affidavit of support for Ifok and he was granted a student visa after he was offered admission to the University of Wisconsin.

Ifok booked his flight with Lufthansa Airlines; he was to have a stop-over in Frankfurt, Germany, spend the night and leave for Chicago, Illinois, the next day. The bellboy at his hotel in Frankfurt offered to provide him with a woman for the night for $100, but Ifok was not interested. Actually, all his thoughts that night were focused on a possible confrontation with the Immigration and Naturalization Service on his arrival in the United States. Some Africans had been denied entry and deported from the country for possessing forged travel documents at various ports of entry within the past year. Immigration and Naturalization officers were, therefore, likely to conduct thorough checks of the documents carried by an African.

Ifok was the only black person on the flight from Frankfurt to Chicago. A movie was shown on the plane and interested passengers had to order headphones for $2 and plug them in in order to get the sound. Ifok ordered a headphone, and was so naïve to think he had purchased it. He, therefore, put it in his bag when the movie ended. An old German lady sitting next to him just stared while he did this. He realized the headphones were on lease when the plane landed in Chicago and all the passengers who had ordered one turned theirs in. Ifok immediately turned his in and avoided being arrested for stealing. He had also bought a bottle of whiskey from the duty-free shop on the plane, and before getting off, drank about half a glassful to calm his nerves.

There were two processing booths at O'Hare Airport: one for American citizens and permanent residents and the other for visitors. Ifok joined the queue leading to the booth for visitors. Just as he had expected, he was singled out for questioning. When it got to his turn, the lady in the booth looked at his visa intently, put it under a microscope and asked him to get out of the line and follow her. She led him straight to the office of Mr Boggart, the head of the airport branch of the Immigration and Naturalization Service. Mr Boggart asked Ifok questions about his last job in Africa and how much money he had for his stay. Ifok showed him a copy of the affidavit of support filed by his American sponsors. Satisfied with the answers given, Mr Boggart himself stamped Ifok's passport and advised him to study hard in school.

CHAPTER 3

Welcome To America

Ifok arrived in the United States three weeks before the beginning of the Fall semester. In Chicago, he stayed with his cousin, Sonny, and did not go out much. Sonny, who had graduated from the University of Wisconsin two years earlier was working two jobs and hardly had the time to take him anywhere, except to see a few African friends. Three days before the beginning of the semester he was joined by Koster, a family friend from Africa who had also been accepted by the University of Wisconsin. Sonny drove Ifok and Koster to the college a day before registration.

ARRIVAL AT
O'HARE AIRPORT,
CHICAGO

On their arrival at the University of Wisconsin in Superior, Wisconsin Ifok and Koster were directed to the residence halls where they were to be assigned rooms. The university had two policies pertaining to housing which Ifok did not like: two students were assigned to each room, and every foreign student had to have an American roommate. After they were assigned rooms, Ifok and Koster decided to go for a walk around campus. This university is a relatively small school and within an hour they had visited every building. After this tour, they decided to look for the nearest tavern and have a drink. After walking for about a quarter of a mile toward the downtown area they got to Bob's Store, where they bought a six-pack of Budweiser beer. They did not know if drinking alcoholic beverages was allowed in the residence halls and did not want to take that chance. They, therefore, went and sat on the lawn near the university's gymnasium drinking their beer. After all, drinking in public was not illegal in their country and they did not think it was illegal in Wisconsin. They spent about an hour and a half hours at this site drinking the beer, and people who walked by stared at them. They in turn thought the people were looking at them because they had seen very few blacks in their lives or were scared of blacks. They did not know people were looking at them because they were breaking the law by drinking in public. As one would expect, someone called the local police and reported them. Fortunately, they were through drinking their beer by the time the police arrived.

"What are you guys doing here?" one of the policemen asked, getting out of his car.

"Just relaxing," Ifok responded.

"And what do you have in that bag?" he asked, reaching for the brown bag with the empty beer cans.

"Garbage" Ifok said.

"You guys are very lucky. If I had seen an opened can among these, I would have taken you straight to jail," the officer concluded.

"Why?" asked Koster.

"Because it is against the law to drink alcoholic beverages in public. This law applies everywhere in this country," the officer said.

"Thank you very much," both Ifok and Koster said.

So, on their first day in Wisconsin they learned something new: drinking in public is prohibited everywhere in America.

When they got to the residence hall, Ifok met his roommate for the first time.

"I am Ifok Hasnem. Pleased to meet you," Ifok said.

"I am Steve Craigo," Steve said.

Nothing was said after these introductory statements. Ifok thought Steve, in his silence, was thinking about sharing the same room with a grown man, a total stranger, from another country. At age 29, and being married and the father of a child, this was a hard arrangement for Ifok to live under. He decided, therefore, to put in a special request for permission to live off-campus.

Registration for the Fall semester was held at the gymnasium the next day. Ifok and Koster were scheduled to register between 2:00 and 3:00 PM. They arrived at the gymnasium by 1:45 PM and by 2:55 PM they had paid their fees and registered for the Fall semester. After this they went for a walk around campus. Seeing a notice for a Black Students' meeting at 5:00 PM, they decided to attend that meeting. Before doing this, they went to Bob's Store and bought a six-pack of beer. This time they took the beer to Ifok's room. They were drinking when Steve came in. He said "Hi", dropped a bag containing his books on his bed and left immediately. He never stayed long enough for Ifok to offer him a beer. Koster jokingly told Ifok he should be careful not to scare the young man to the point of getting a heart attack.

There were only nine students present—all of them Black Americans—when Ifok and Koster arrived at the meeting. They wondered why there were no other Africans present; after all most Africans are black. They reasoned that maybe the Africans on campus had not seen the notice for the meeting. Around 5:15 PM, about ten more Black American students came in. After everyone signed in, the president asked all present to introduce themselves. The atmosphere was tense when Ifok and Koster introduced themselves; they had a feeling something was wrong. After the introductions, the president announced that the meeting had been cancelled and would be held at a later date. The president did not give a reason for the cancellation, but it seemed everyone present, with the exception of Ifok and Koster, agreed with him. Later, other Africans on campus informed Ifok and Koster that Africans were not members of the Black Students Union, and that it was probably because of their presence that the meeting was cancelled.

Ifok's request for permission to live off-campus was granted by the director of housing within a week. He rented a room at 40 Nowind Avenue for $40 a week; he had cooking privileges and could also use the landlady's washing machine and dryer. After about a month, he purchased the landlady's 1961 Ford for $100. 40 Nowind Avenue was about a mile from campus and Ifok needed a car for the cold months ahead; additionally, he needed a car if he was really serious in his quest for a job, on or off campus.

About half-way through the fall semester, Ifok got a job with the food service section on campus as a cleaner/dishwasher at the rate of $2 an hour. He worked ten hours a week between 5:00 and 7:00 PM, Monday through Friday. He needed the money so that, within a short time, he would be able to afford an air ticket for his wife as planned.

Working as a cleaner/dishwasher was not easy for Ifok, maybe because of his background and experiences. The last job he held in Africa was that of district head of a government department. Now here he was, in the United States, working virtually as a servant. It really bothered him and he thought it was a disgrace to his family.

To conceal his identity, he wore a large hat and dark glasses while at work. He especially worried of being recognized by other Africans who had government scholarships and did not need an extra buck. With the passage of time, however, he became less and less shy and paranoid about his part-time job and stopped wearing his disguise to work. He reasoned that he should rather be proud and congratulate himself for having the courage and the willingness to do almost anything to make a living in this country; after all, he was not American.

Ifok's life during the average week consisted of classes during the day, work during the early evening and study at night. On Friday nights, Ifok and Koster would get together by 8:00 PM, drink till about 10:30 PM, and go out, usually to a club called The Cave to look for dates. The easiest women to pick up, with the least opposition from young white males, were women in their thirties and forties, usually divorced and a little heavy. These women also appealed to Ifok because they did not expect their dates to spend a lot of money and were not looking for serious relationships. The foundation for any such liaison was built of sex, and sex with consenting adults was what Ifok and Koster wanted. One-night-stands were always welcome.

One Friday night in early Spring 1975, Ifok and Koster went to The Cave very drunk. They got a table and ordered some drinks. Right next to their table was this woman; white, blonde, and aged about forty. Ifok went over and asked her for a dance and she agreed. "My name is Betty and I have lived in this area all my life", she said.

"Your accent tells me that you are not American. Wait. Don't tell me where you're from. I will guess. You are from Jamaica?" she asked.

"No" Ifok said.

"From the Bahamas?" she asked.

"No" Ikof said.

"From India?" she asked. Ikof laughed at the thought of being considered an Asian Indian.

"No. I am African" Ikof said.

"Wow. An African! You are the first African I have met. I have been told Africans are very nice people" Betty said.

"I am the nicest of them all" Ifok joked.

After dancing with Betty, Ifok asked her if he and Koster could join her at her table and she said they could. In more talks with her, Ikof found out she was a widow, and alumnus of the University Ifok and Koster were attending, and was currently employed as the director of a social service agency in the city. Ifok and Koster danced with Betty till the club closed at 3:00am and she invited them to her home for an early morning breakfast.

After breakfast, Betty invited Ifok to her bedroom where he made love to her. After spending about thirty minutes with her she told him she wanted Koster to also make love to her. Koster was a little hesitant because he thought that Ifok would probably like to keep Betty as a girlfriend. Ifok told him to forget about what was proper and take care of business. "You cannot make a girlfriend out of a woman who also wants to sleep with your friend," Ifok stressed to Koster. Satisfied that his action would not offend Ifok, Koster also made love to Betty and the two of them stayed with her until 2:00 PM. Before leaving Betty's house they exchanged phone numbers and she asked them to come back anytime for a good time. Ifok and

Koster never went back together to Betty's house; they made individual visits. Betty was always able to satisfy their sexual needs. Later, she introduced them to three of her friends who had such interest in younger men. She was very kind to them.

There were over 120 African students enrolled at the University of Wisconsin in 1974. Of this number only 12 were Ifok's compatriots; and only one in that group had a government scholarship while the rest were being sponsored by their families or they were working and paying their way in school. The majority of the remaining Africans were on full scholarships from their governments and they lived well and drove nice cars. Ifok learned that some of these students had very wealthy parents who could afford to send them extra funds to maintain the lifestyle they had enjoyed at home.

Ifok could not afford such a lifestyle with his meager resources. He and Koster purchased their winter coats at a resale store and their regular clothes from Sears Roebuck. On the advice of his landlady, Ifok and Koster attended her church, The Presbyterian Church in town, where the officiating clergyman, Pastor John Piper was very nice to them. On their first day at the church, Pastor Piper announced that he was welcoming two visitors who were new arrivals in the United States, and urged his congregation to donate any used items which Ifok and Koster could still use. After the service, Pastor Piper asked Ifok and Koster to stand by him at the church entrance and shake the hands of the worshipers as they left. The church members were very nice to them that day and on subsequent visits. Later, Pastor Piper brought them used winter clothing of higher quality than those they had purchased at the resale store. He also arranged the snow shoveling of the driveways of some senior citizens for pay.

By the end of Summer 1975, Ifok had saved enough money to afford an air ticket for his wife. Since he had all her educational particulars, he enrolled her at the Vocational Training Center in town for the certificate program in fashion merchandising. He paid the semester's fees of $200 and sent her a copy of the receipt that she could use to apply for a student visa. His wife's father, who also had accounts in New York and London, also sent sworn statements to the United States Embassy indicating his willingness to support his daughter. Gama finally arrived in the United States on January 6, 1976, on a student visa.

At the airport, Ifok felt his wife was not happy. She did not seem enthused about seeing him after a period of eighteen months. When she gave him a passionless kiss, Ifok knew there was something seriously missing in their marriage. He reasoned that whatever the problems were, they would be able to overcome them. His wife hardly talked to him and that was very unusual of her.

Gama started classes at her school a week after her arrival. She registered for four courses—English, Mathematics, Typing, and Sociology—and Ifok promised to help her with her school work if she had any problems. Although Gama did everything a wife would do, Ifok still felt there was something missing in their marriage and that she was not happy despite her claims to the contrary. Monday through Friday, Ifok would drive her to school in the morning and pick her in the early afternoon; they would have lunch together and then Ifok would go to work in the evening after a nap. After about three weeks, he realized that all Gama did in her spare time was watch television; she never did her school assignments and that made him very upset. He felt that there was the need for them to have a serious talk, and this took place one evening after dinner.

Gama told Ifok that she did not think their marriage was going to work out because his parents did not like her, and that his mother was very hostile to her after he left the country.

"About a month after you left the country, I took Rojo to your house to see your parents but I was told they were asleep. It was in the early evening, the time they usually had their tea in the gazebo. After about an hour of waiting, your dad came out to talk with us and play with Rojo. He asked me when I was planning on joining you and I told him that would be in about a year. Your mom joined us later but had to leave for a scheduled appointment. Before leaving for her appointment, she advised me to bring Rojo again two weeks later which I did, but she was not in. Once again, it was your dad who entertained us," Gama said.

Ifok was silent on hearing what Gama said. He had always been aware that his mother did not care much for Gama's mother, and her stepfather who was a white man. Gama's mother had married him after her divorce from Gama's father. They both smoked cigarettes, a habit Adeye abhorred. Additionally, Gama's mother usually wore slacks which were considered western attire and frowned upon by older folks.

"After those two visits, I never took Rojo to your parents' house anymore because they did not show much interest in us. Five months later, your parents' driver dropped off some items you had purchased in America for Rojo. They had not called to let me know the driver was coming but I called later to let them know I had received the items. A day before my departure to this country I went to your parents' house to say goodbye, and they did not give me anything to bring to you. I told them Rojo would be staying with my parents till he joined us. That was what happened after you left," Gama said.

"Also, I do not think I can stay in this country for as long as you have planned. I think there is too much suffering here," she said.

"Why did you not write to tell me about all this before you left Africa?" Ifok asked.

"I don't know. I had wanted to but I felt it would be better for me to come over here and let you know how I felt," she said.

"Okay, I will grant your wish if that is what you want. I will suggest, however, that you leave at the end of this semester so that I can avoid answering embarrassing questions by our friends. If you leave at the end of this semester, I can always tell people that you have gone home for the summer and that you will be coming back with Rojo before the beginning of the Fall semester. I will graduate in summer and leave for Chicago, and no one will know whether you come back or not," Ifok said.

"That sounds nice. I am glad you understand me. I shall write to my mother so that she will send me an air ticket for my flight home. Do you think I should continue going to school until I leave?" Gama asked.

"Yes, I think you should," Ifok said. "And I shall do all your homework for you, if possible, till the end of the semester," Ifok concluded.

After this candid conversation and decision about their marriage, Gama's attitude changed and she became her real self. Ifok decided to treat her nice till her departure. In addition to working and his school work, he did her homework for her. Her parents sent her an air ticket together with about $400 for shopping, and Ifok drove her around to buy things she wanted to take home. About two weeks before Gama was to leave,

Ifok gave his close friends, Koster and Jeffrey, the bad news. They were very surprised and wanted to know why. All he told them was that the conditions which existed at the beginning of their marriage no longer did so they decided to go their separate ways.

On the day of Gama's departure, Ifok drove her to the airport. He wished her the best of luck in her future endeavors and urged her to take good care of their son. She in turn advised Ifok to quit drinking alcohol. That same night, Ifok went to The Cave to cool off after the nerve-racking experience of the past four months. He had two drinks, did not dance and left for home at about 12:30 AM. When he got home, he laid on his bed and started thinking about his short marriage, his wife's four-month stay in this country, his future, and his son, He finally said to himself: "Life must continue. There is nothing I can do to change the past!"

CHAPTER 4

The Big City

Ifok graduated from the University of Wisconsin with honors. His plan was to leave for the big city, Chicago, to work for a year, save some money, and go to graduate school. He called an African friend, Eneo, who lived and worked in Chicago as a cab driver, and Eneo agreed he could come and stay with him while he looked for a job. He settled for Eneo because his cousin, Sonny, no longer lived in Chicago; he had moved to Louisville, Kentucky. With the arrangements for his stay in Chicago made, Ifok decided to stay in Wisconsin and have a good time with Betty until the beginning of the Fall semester. He sold his 1961 Ford and bought a 1965 VW Bug, because the Bug is cheaper on gas and he anticipated cash flow problems.

Ifok left for Chicago at 9:00 AM. He had prepared some sandwiches for lunch during the 6-hour trip. He had also bought a six-pack of coca cola, so with the sandwiches he was set for his trip. His plan was to avoid stopping at any small town. Any stop was to be at a gas station by the highway to buy gas and/or to use the bathroom. The rationale for this was for him to avoid contact with rural white folks and police who, he suspected, would be more prejudiced because they had had fewer contacts with blacks. He also obeyed all the highway signs and never went beyond the posted 55 MPH speed limit. Despite this, he was followed by local police on two occasions; they probably stopped trailing him after he left their jurisdictions. Ifok made only one stop during the trip, to buy gas and use the washroom. By the time he got out of the bathroom, two policemen had driven up to the station and were talking to the manager. Ifok looked their way in order to say "Hi" but they quickly turned their heads. He walked to his car and quickly left for the interstate highway.

Ifok arrived in Chicago during the evening rush hour, and had to increase his driving speed to cope with the traffic flow. He followed the directions Eneo gave him and within a very short time he was at the house of Ms Hambles, Eneo's former mother-in-law. Eneo had promised to be there by 6:00 PM to take him to his apartment. Ms Hambles fixed Ifok something to eat and after that he watched television while waiting for Eneo. When he had not shown up by 9:30 PM, Ms Hambles asked her son, Elbert, to help Ifok unload his things from his car and bring them in so that he could spend the night with the family. Eneo arrived at Mrs Hambles house at about 10:00 PM, just after Elbert and Ifok were through bringing his things into the house. They re-loaded his things into his car, and he drove and followed Eneo's taxi to his apartment which was about three miles away.

When they arrived at Eneo's apartment, Ifok found out that Eneo was living with Elsie, a lady he claimed used to be a very close friend of his ex-wife. The only furniture in the apartment was a mattress on the floor on which Eneo and Elsie slept. The apartment was a very small studio and Ifok slept on the floor of the bathroom. That did not bother him so long as it did not bother Eneo and Elsie. Every evening, Ifok would buy a copy of the next day's issue of the Chicago Tribune and select the job positions he would be applying for in the morning. Eneo also helped by giving him directions to places of employment. Some advertised positions required applicants to call; in such cases, Ifok made the calls from a pay phone in front of Eneo's apartment building because Eneo did not have a phone. Within the first three weeks of his stay, Ifok applied for over thirty positions but was not hired for any of them. With the passage of time, he realized that Eneo's attitude towards him was changing.

During the first week of his stay, Ifok bought groceries and cooked. In the evenings when Eneo returned from work, the two of them would drink some beer before having dinner. Eneo would tell him the easiest job was cab driving and that he would help him get hired at his garage if he wished. Ifok was afraid to drive a cab because cab drivers were easy targets for stick-up men, and he did not know his way around the city. His unwillingness to drive a cab might have angered Eneo since he was doing the same thing for a living; he probably might have felt that that a guy in Ifok's situation should take any job irrespective of the risks.

By the end of the second week, Ifok had run out of money and Eneo was buying the groceries. Before going to work, he would give Elsie or Ifok some money, and one of them would go to the store, buy the necessary items and do the cooking. In the evenings, Eneo would come home later than usual and as high as a kite, eat and go straight to bed; the guy would hardly talk to Ifok. By the third week, Eneo was not buying food regularly and Ifok had to depend on other friends for his livelihood. Around 7:00 PM every day, Eneo would come home, take Elsie out, Ifok assumed, to a restaurant to eat since none of them ate in his presence any longer. For the first time in his life, Ifok went for a whole day without food.

During the fourth week his car broke down and he sold it for $100. He used about $30 to buy groceries for the house which Eneo and Elsie heartily enjoyed. He responded to an advertisement in the newspaper for a personnel assistant and was invited for an interview.

"Why did you apply for this position? The personnel director asked.

"I applied for the position because I have the necessary qualifications and experience and I believe I can do a good job," Ifok replied.

"How long have you been in this country?" the director asked.

"Two years" Ifok resonded.

"And those two years have been spent in school," she said. "I also see that your relevant work experiences have been outside this country," she continued.

"Yes" Ifok said.

"Do you have a green card? She asked. The green card is the work permit required of all aliens who are permanent residents of the United States.

"No, I just applied for one," Ifok replied. He had lied though. "I will get in contact with the Immigration and Naturalization Service and get a statement to the effect that I am authorized to work, pending approval of my application," Ifok continued.

"Okay. Just bring me such a letter and you have a job. Good luck to you," she said.

"Thank you very much," Ifok said.

Ifok left this company knowing fully well that he was not going there again. He had a student visa which did not authorize him to work. He felt sorry for giving the personnel director all that information about himself. He hoped the personnel director would not make a report to the Immigration and Naturalization Service about his attempt to get a job.

Rafael, another African who knew one of Ifok's elder brothers back home, rented an apartment in Eneo's building. When Ifok told him of what he was going through, Rafael told him to move in with him until he found a job. Rafael lived alone and worked on the second shift from 3:00 to 11:00 PM. The only times Ifok could not stay at Rafael's apartment were on Friday and Saturday nights when his girlfriend, Lucy, came to stay overnight. On such occasions, Ifok spent the night on Chicago Transit Authority (CTA) trains till the morning. Anyway, Eneo was glad to get rid of Ifok when he told him of Rafael's offer. After he moved to Rafael's place, Ifok scarcely saw Eneo, although they lived in the same building. A month later, Eneo moved, Ifok was told, to the northern part of the city; he never told Ifok he was moving and did not give him his new address. Evidently, he did not want Ifok to bother him anymore!

AUTO PORTER

While he was staying with Rafael, Ifok met Jim, another African who worked as an auto porter for a Ford dealership. Jim told Ifok that his supervisor had informed him he wanted to fire John, another auto porter, for perpetual drunkenness and he would like Jim to get one of his African friends to take up that position when it became available. Ifok told Jim he would be interested in such a position. Two weeks after this conversation, Jim called Ifok and gave him directions to his place of work so that he could apply for the position. On the application he lied about his education and work experience: he did not state that he had a college degree and he claimed to have worked as an auto porter for three years in Africa. Ifok was hired for the position and was asked to start working the next day at the rate of $4 an hour, which was about a dollar and one-half over the minimum wage. Ifok was so happy that day he drank like a fish. He gave Rafael the good news when he came home from work that day, and promised to rent his own apartment after he received his second paycheck.

On his first day at work, the supervisor, Mr Moses, asked Jim to train Ifok on what the job entailed, since he would be doing the same work as Jim. They started by sweeping and cleaning all the offices, mopping floors where necessary and emptying all trash cans. They then wiped the dust from all the cars on display in the showroom, after which they went outside and put the keys in the ignitions of the over 100 new cars parked on the two-acre lot of the company. After this they came to the main garage where they mainly cleaned new cars thoroughly—bumpers, tires, floors, windshields etc.—as they were sold. When there were no new cars to clean, they were assigned duties like scrubbing walls, cleaning washrooms and outside windows, and sweeping the company lot and the alley behind the establishment. All of the above constituted what an auto porter did at this dealership. Ifok felt that was too much work for the $135 he was taking home each week. After being on the job for one week, Jim asked Ifok if he liked the job and he told him the truth, which was that they were being abused; they were being paid very little money for so much work. He told Jim he would leave as soon as he found another job, and Jim was disappointed; Jim felt Ifok was being too choosy.

Ifok tried to understand Jim's reasoning because their backgrounds were completely different. Jim had had only six years of formal education and was ready to take any job regardless of the pay. Ifok was ready to do any job at the right price. Jim also felt that because he told Ifok of the job opening, Ifok owed him something. When Ifok received his first paycheck, Jim told him to buy some liquor for their supervisor as a symbol of appreciation for having offered him the job. Although Ifok did not like that idea, he did as Jim advised and bought the pint of whiskey for the supervisor.

He also bought Jim a $10 bag of marijuana and a pack of cigarettes. Despite this, Jim kept on making unreasonable demands of him. On an average week, Ifok would buy him, at least, two packs of cigarettes, and would share his lunch with him, at least, once. Ifok decided to put a stop to this nonsense after his first month on the job. By then he had left Rafael's house and moved to his own apartment.

Jim asked Ifok to give him a $10 loan one Monday morning.

"Say, Ifok. I need a $10 loan," Jim said.

"When are you going to pay it back? Ifok asked.

"Wow! You can be so mean sometimes," Jim said.

"I am not being mean. I am being honest. I want to know when you will pay it back so that I will give it to you if I can afford to," Ifok said.

"Okay, I will give your money to you on Friday as soon as we receive our pay," Jim replied. With this promise, Ifok gave Jim the $10.

Ifok expected Jim to give him the money as soon as he received his check on Friday, but Jim did not. Ifok asked him for the money on Monday and Jim told him he could not pay him because he had to make some unexpected expenses during the weekend. Jim promised to effect payment of the loan the following Friday, and he did. After this Jim did not talk to Ifok anymore but this did not bother Ifok because their views about what was proper behavior were poles apart. Later, Ifok learned from Rafael that Jim was expecting Ifok to reward him for having helped him obtain the job.

Three weeks later, Ifok was fired. It happened on a payday. Before Mr Moss handed Ifok his check, he told him the reason for his dismissal.

"Do you have a college degree? Mr Moss asked.

"No. May I know why you are asking me that? Ifok asked.

"Anyway, I have learnt from a very reliable source that you have a college degree and that you do not intend to keep this job for long. I want someone who will stay here for as long as possible. And you do not look like such a person," he continued.

"I am surprised at your reason for my dismissal," Ifok said.

"Anyway, I think you are overqualified for the position, and you are fired.

Ifok, as was his habit, thanked Mr Moss and left his office, disappointed because he would have to struggle hard to find another job but happy because the exploitation of his labor was over.

Although Ifok had enough money to pay his rent and survive for, at least, two months, he did not rest on his oars; he started looking for work immediately. After looking for about two weeks, he realized that because he did not have a green card or work permit he was going to have a hard time in getting a decent job. On two occasions, he lost job offers because he could not produce a green card. He became very depressed and scared because these employers had information about him which they could report to the Immigration and Naturalization Service. From then on, anytime Ifok was at a public place and saw a white man dressed in a suit he feared he could be an immigration officer looking for him. He opened his door only to people who had called earlier to let him know they were coming to visit. He wanted to move but could not because he did not have a job, and no sane landlord would allow an unemployed guy to sign a lease for an apartment.

After being unsuccessful in obtaining employment in three weeks, Ifok decided to become a cab driver. There were dangers involved, but the cab companies did not ask for a green card or work permit. He applied at Dagger Cab Company on the south side and was hired after he made the $100 bond deposit. He was told to report for work the next day. That night he could not sleep: he laid in bed thinking about being robbed, shot at and killed, or being arrested by the Immigration and Naturalization Service and deported to Africa. He decided to drive his cab only in areas he was familiar with. His plan was to avoid danger and just make a few bucks each day.

When Ifok arrived at the cab company on his first day of work, he was trembling all over. After he was allocated a cab, he decided to go home and eat breakfast before starting to work. When he got to the first traffic light, about a block from the garage, he was flagged down by two black men whose very appearance scared the hell out of him. They had on long coats underneath which they could hide anything from a hammer to a pistol. Although Ifok had the "Not For Hire" sign on, they tried to force their way into his cab. Ifok took off immediately although he had the red light, and nearly caused an accident.

When he arrived home, he fixed some eggs and sausages to eat but he really did not have much of an appetite. He, however, forced himself to eat half of what he had prepared. As he got ready to leave the house, he had a funny feeling in his throat. He rushed to the bathroom where he vomited everything he had eaten. His body could not hold any food because of fear of what was ahead that day!

He got his first ride near his house. A middle-aged black man flagged him down and he stopped. "Union Station," he said, as soon as he entered the cab.

"I am sorry, Sir. I do not know how to get there from here, and you will have to give me directions," Ifok said.

"That is just west of the Loop, at Adams and Canal. Anyway, I will give you directions," the passenger said. On their way to his destination, the passenger advised Ifok to work in the Loop and avoid the south side of the city, where he said some people would take advantage of him because of his lack of knowledge of the city. At the end of the trip, the passenger added a dollar tip to the fare and wished Ifok good luck. Despite the passenger's advice, Ifok returned to the south side. He knew that part was dangerous, but he lived there and was more familiar with that area than the downtown area. Additionally, the Immigration and Naturalization Service did not have an office on the south side, and that took out some of the fear while he worked in that part of the city. Ifok's net income on his first day was $10; within two weeks, he was averaging $25 a day.

Driving a cab provided Ifok with new and unexpected experiences. Some passengers talked about their personal and professional lives; and some female passengers became his girlfriends. On one occasion, a female passenger asked him to have sex with her on the backseat of his cab, confessing she had fantasies about sleeping with strangers she never expected to see again. Another passenger confessed having a crush on the natives in Tarzan movies; her wish was to have a few of them bathed and sprinkled with cologne before having sexual intercourse with her. On two occasions he had no choice but to accept food stamps in lieu of cash or nothing at all. He was never robbed at gun point in the cab. On a few occasions, however, some passengers cleverly outwitted him and did not pay for the ride. He had his first experience with non-payment of fare one Friday afternoon when he picked up a couple at 18th and State Street. The man told Ifok that they were going to 78th and Exchange Street on the south side. When they arrived at this destination, a courtyard building, the man asked the woman to go upstairs to get the money for the fare. When the woman did not return after about fifteen minutes, the guy told Ifok he was leaving his parcel with him as a guarantee that he would return with the money; by the time the man left, the cab meter had registered $14. When none of them returned after about thirty minutes, Ifok drove off thinking the parcel might contain something valuable he could sell to make up for the fare. He found out the parcel contained old newspapers. On another occasion, Ifok's passenger, a black man who appeared drunk, asked him to go to his apartment with him to get his money. "You have to come with me if you want to get paid," he said. When Ifok refused, the man walked away without paying for the ride.

One day Ifok picked up a passenger who threatened to seize the cab because Ifok did not appear to know his way around town. When Ifok did not take the route the passenger had in mind the passenger became very irate.

"Where are you going?" the passenger asked.

"Ashland and Belmont, as you requested," Ifok said.

"That's not how you get to Ashland and Belmont from here? Who gave you this cab? I have every right to seize it," he continued.

"Cool it, Sir. I am taking you by the route I know," Ifok said, stopping the cab and turning off the meter.

"Now, give me directions and I will take you to your destination," Ifok said. "You can get out of the cab if you are no longer interested in the ride," Ifok concluded.

The passenger was taken aback by Ifok's exhibition of anger, and respectfully directed Ifok to his destination. Ifok had taken charge. At the end of the trip the passenger paid the exact fare and slammed the door.

Since he was determined to start graduate studies at Eastern Illinois University in Charleston, Illinois, Ifok tried to save as much of his earnings as he could; on the average, he saved about $150 a month. He had two lovers who satisfied his sexual needs when he provided them with alcohol, marijuana and a few dollars. Evidently, he looked like a fool to Tree, one of his lovers who did not waste time to steal things from his apartment whenever she got the opportunity. During the period of their relationship which lasted for about four months, she stole his watch, bankbook, and wooden hair pick.

Tree got the chance to steal Ifok's watch when he left her alone in his apartment and went to the next building to talk to a friend whose phone had been disconnected. He was gone for just about ten minutes, but that was long enough for Tree to do a number on the watch. A few minutes after Ifok returned, Tree decided to leave so that she could take her kids to their grandmother's house, she claimed. Ifok realized his watch was missing later that night. He called Tree's number but there was no response. Tree, on her part, did not call Ifok for three days. On the fourth day when she came to Ifok's apartment and Ifok asked her about the watch, she stated she had not seen it. Despite what had happened, Ifok made love to Tree that day. He needed sex, and sex with Tree was always excellent. He was, however, very alert anytime she was around. He needed a third eye for that, like they say in Chicago.

Tree managed to steal Ifok's bankbook and wooden hair pick about a month later. On that day Tree came to Ifok's apartment with a white girl named Snow. She summoned Ifok to the bathroom where she told him he could have sex with Snow if he gave her (Tree) $5. Ifok told Tree he had only $3. Tree took the money and ordered Snow to take off her clothes so that Ifok would have sex with her. Tree went to the bathroom while Ifok was making love to Snow, and it was probably during that time that Tree hid the wooden hair pick somewhere on her body. Tree probably had the opportunity to take Ifok's savings bankbook from his drawer when he went to the bathroom after making love to Snow.

Anyway, Ifok realized both items were missing the next day. He made a report to the bank, and his account number was changed and he was given a new bankbook. He also decided to break up his strange relationship with Tree. He called her that evening and told her to not call or come to his house anymore and hung up. She complied and never bothered Ifok again.

CHAPTER 5

Small Town Living/ Back To School

Ifok received his letter of admission to the graduate school at Eastern Illinois University for the Fall semester in early July; the semester was to start at the end of August. He was disappointed though, because he was not offered any of the assistantships or scholarships he had applied for and he had not saved enough money for his expenses while in school. He had saved only $1,200, out of which he used $300 to purchase a 1970 VW Bug. He decided to go to Charleston to pay $400 toward his first semester's tuition, get a part-time job and pay the rest of the fees in installments.

He planned to visit Charleston two weeks before the beginning of the semester for two main reasons: first, to look for an apartment and second, to take some of his things, mainly books, a stereo set, and a television. For this trip, he decided to use his cab instead of his car. Two of his friends, Alex and Richard, agreed to go with him on this trip. He called another friend, Muuta, who was also a graduate student at Charleston and told him of his planned visit. Muuta assured Ifok that he could leave his things at his apartment if he could not have an apartment to rent during his visit.

Ifok and his friends went on this trip on a Saturday. They left Chicago at 9:00 AM and got to Charleston by 1:00 PM. They were stopped and questioned on two occasions by local police. After all, a Chicago cab loaded with personal belongings and three black men in it should be of interest to any policeman. In Charleston, Ifok made a few calls to some landlords and they were either not home or their rents were too high. Muuta told Ifok he could stay with him for the first two weeks of the semester while he looked for an appartment. With this assurance, Ifok left his things at Muuta's apartment and returned to Chicago with Alex and Richard.

He returned to Charleston with the rest of his belongings the day before registration for the Fall semester. The next day, he went to the Accounts Office at the university at about 9:00 AM to arrange a schedule of payment of his fees for the semester. He was informed he would not be allowed to register till he paid the semester's fees in full. Since he did not have that much money, he was confronted with two options. The first was to stay in Charleston, look for a job and start school in the Spring semester; the second was to return to Chicago. Ifok chose the former alternative and started looking for a job. Three days after classes started, he received a note from the Foreign Student Advisor, Ms Landers, asking him to be in touch with her immediately. She was aware of his problem and Ifok had a gut feeling his meeting with her would result in something good.

"Have you been able to find a job?" she asked Ifok as soon as he entered her office.

"No, not yet but I am sure I will find one very soon," Ifok answered.

"Well, then I have good news for you. I can award you a scholarship for this semester. I have examined your transcript and you appear to be an excellent student. You are to take a minimum of 12 credit hours this semester and the scholarship will be extended only if you get a minimum grade point average of 3.00," she said.

"Thank you very much, Ms Landers. I will study hard to keep this scholarship and graduate by Summer next year," Ifok said.

"And keep this in mind. Some foreign students have abused this scholarship program by taking full-time jobs and not devoting enough time to their studies to earn good grades. I hope you will not disappoint me," Ms Landers said.

"I will not disappoint you," Ifok promised.

Ms Landers gave Ifok a clearance certificate which he took to the Registrar's Office where he registered for the semester. Two weeks after he started classes, he got a part-time job as a dishwasher at a hotel in a city just west of Charleston. He was paid $2.50 an hour and worked a maximum of twenty hours a week. The main advantage of this job was the free food he had anytime he went to work. He moved from Muuta's apartment and rented a new one with Joseph, another African; his portion of the rent was $100 a month.

Social life in Charleston consisted mainly of visits to night clubs, theatres, bars, and private parties. Ifok never really had the time to participate much in the above because he was always studying, attending classes, working or sleeping. In all, he was invited to about seven private parties during his one-year stay in Charleston, but he attended just two of them; on those occasions the few friends he had were surprised to see him there. He never went to any night clubs and theatres. As far as sexual relations were concerned he had three lovers: two black students named Barbara and Benita and aged 18 and 25 respectively, and a 40-year old white woman named Lilian. He usually spent time with one of these women every weekend, Benita and Lilian in their houses, and Barbara, in his apartment since she had two roommates. All three women were aware that Ifok's relationship with them was mainly physical. Barbara, the youngest, was the one who bothered him with her money problems sometimes. Money was out as far as Benita and Lilian were concerned. In fact, Benita gave Ifok $100 on one occasion when he did not have enough money to pay his rent.

Ifok made good grades during his first semester and his scholarship was extended to cover the second semester. He also had a scholarship for the summer session; by then he needed just six credits to graduate and could take a chance by indulging more in the social activities in Charleston. On the last day of the second semester, he had the chance to talk with the woman he was to marry, Zenny. He had seen her on campus on a number of occasions but never had the opportunity to talk with her and they did not have common friends. On this day, he saw her walking in the direction he was driving; he summoned enough courage, pulled to a stop and offered her a ride. She was going to the administrative services building on campus so he drove her there; they exchanged phone numbers.

Ifok called her that same night and they talked. He found out that Zenny was 29 years old, divorced and had two children aged 11 and 9. Ifok told her he was also divorced and had a 6-year old son, although he had by then not received his final divorce decree from Africa. Zenny told him that she would be leaving for Chicago the next day and would be back in two weeks to attend summer school. Ifok told her he might go to Chicago himself and she gave him a number to contact her on. He, however, did not go to Chicago; rather he worked longer hours at his job and made more money during the brief break.

Zenny called Ifok as soon as she returned to Charleston and they started going steady. Within about three weeks, he moved in with her since he was already spending most nights at her house. Zenny and Ifok had a very nice summer together. On weekday mornings, they would all go to school for about two hours; in the evenings, Ifok would go to work. On weekends, they would either go to the movies or drive to the park near Lake Charleston for a mini picnic. Two weeks before the end of the summer session, Ifok received a check for $1,000 from his father. He resigned from his dishwasher job because he planned to move to Chicago after his graduation which was less than three weeks away. His VW broke down a week later and he decided to junk it instead of fixing it because its body was too rusted. He sold it for $75 and purchased a 1965 Chevrolet Impala. The Impala had only 36,000 on the odometer, and according to the owner had not been driven during the past five years. Ifok paid only $150 for that car.

Ifok graduated with a Master of Arts degree in August, 1978. Although he ordered the cap and gown, he changed his mind at the last minute and did not attend the convocation. He celebrated with Zenny by drinking beer and wine. Together, Ifok and Zenny made plans for the future: they would move to Chicago and get married; she would stay with her relatives and Ifok would stay with a friend till one of them found a job; then they would rent an apartment and she would continue her schooling on part-time basis. Meanwhile, Ifok had saved $500 which they could use as security deposit and first month's rent.

CHAPTER 6

Back To The Big City

Zenny and Ifok got married about two weeks after their arrival in Chicago. Ifok did not want to drive a cab again because he still considered it a dangerous job. He got a job as a security guard about a week after their marriage and they rented a one-bedroom apartment on the north side of the city. This position reminded him of the "night watchmen" who guarded his family home in Africa. He worked from 3:00 PM to 11:00 PM and Zenny always prepared sandwiches for him to eat at work; and there was also always food for him to eat on his arrival home from work. Ifok continued his search for a better job by preparing a resume which he sent out in response to advertised positions for which he was qualified.

Working as a security guard was not easy; it involved more than Ifok thought. On his first day at his post, a factory in Carol Stream, Illinois, Mr Maller, his supervisor told him there had been bomb threats at the plant within the past month.

"What should I do when I receive such a call? Ifok asked.

"First, you get on the intercom and advise all employees in the building to get out of the premises. Then you call the local police and fire departments. Then you call me," Mr Maller said.

"I guess I should do the same in case of a fire," Ifok said.

"Yes, but in that case you should get a fire extinguisher and start putting out the fire immediately," said Mr Miller.

He then proceeded to show Ifok how to use a fire extinguisher. As Ifok listened to Mr Miller, he hoped that during his stay on this job nothing would necessitate his having to go through any of the above routines.

One day during his third week on the job, at about 8:00 PM, Ifok received a phone call that three bombs had been planted in the premises and that one of them was in the washroom next to the security office. The first thing Ifok did was to run to his car. After he got to his car, he then remembered everything Mr Maller had told him to do under such circumstances. He finally summoned enough courage, went back into the building and called the local police and fire departments from a pay phone located about ten yards from the security office. He run out of the building and back to his car as soon as he was through making his calls. The police and fire officials arrived in about ten minutes and did not find any bombs after a thorough search. He called Mr Maller after these official left and was surprised he did not complain about his actions. Anyway, after this incident Ifok intensified his efforts in search of another job. He got one six weeks later as an assembler, a job which paid a dollar more an hour and did not entail the frightening situations a security guard had to face sometimes.

SECURITY GUARD

Meanwhile, around this time, Ifok and Zenny had started encountering problems in their marriage. Zenny's best friend, Tammy, who had recently been separated from her husband, rented an apartment in their building. After this, Zenny hardly spent anytime in their apartment. In six months, Ifok could count the number of times both he and his wife went to bed at the same time. Once, he told his wife of openings at the factory where he worked, and she replied she was not interested because the wages were too low. Ifok was offended because that was how he made his living then. Later, Zenny applied for a Pell Grant and enrolled at Truman College on the north side of the city. After this, she started spending all her weekday evenings and nights outside; she usually came home in the early hours of the morning. Whenever Ifok asked her why she came home so late she replied she had been at Tammy's apartment. If Zenny wanted their marriage to continue under such conditions, Ifok reasoned, then she was crazy!

Ifok was laid off from his job as an assembler after just about a month. Because he did not work for more than six weeks, he was not eligible for unemployment benefits. Later, he learned the company hired more workers to fill an order for the Christmas holidays and laid them off after filling it. He decided to start driving a cab again, this time, for Red Cab Company while he looked for a better job.

He went to the employment office of Red Cab Company and filled out an application. Mr Putt, the personnel officer, advised Ifok to call him after one week to find out if there were openings in any of the garages. Ifok called Mr Putt after a week and Mr Putt told him there were no openings. Later, he learned, Mr Putt would not hire him unless he gave a bribe. An African friend told him he gave Mr Putt a $50 bribe before he was hired. Armed with this information, Ifok went to the employment office of Red Cab Company with $50 in a sealed envelope addressed to Mr Putt. He waited in the hallway until Mr Putt was alone in the office and then went in to take care of business.

"This is for you to buy some drinks with," Ifok said, handing the envelope to Mr Putt who grabbed it and put it in his coat pocket. "I have a wife and kids, and I need a job so that I can take care of them," Ifok continued.

Mr Putt asked for Ifok's last name and when Ifok told him, he looked through a stack of applications on his desk but could not find Ifok's.

"Well, I cannot find your application so I will give you a new one to fill out," he said.

He gave Ifok a new application and left him alone in the office, most probably to go to the washroom to count the money. There was a satisfied look on Mr Putt's face when he returned to the office. Ifok was hired and he started driving the next day.

His approach to cab-driving this time was different. He operated mainly on the north side, downtown, and O'Hare Airport because he now had a permanent resident visa and was therefore not afraid of being apprehended by the immigration authorities. He worked very hard and always came by enough money to meet the monthly obligations of his family. With time, Zenny got a job as a social service assistant at a home for mentally handicapped adults at a weekly wage of $135. Ifok and Zenny agreed she would spend $200 a month on food while he took care of all the other monthly expenses. This arrangement worked well during the first month. The second month, Zenny bought $160 worth of groceries; by the third month she had reduced this expenditure to about $120. Ifok decided not to complain but rather to have his meals in restaurants anytime there was not enough food in the house. He felt that if Zenny really cared for her children, she would change her mind and spend as much as originally planned. His strategy worked and within a month Zenny started buying enough food for the house.

Ifok had a very traumatic experience while driving his cab. It all started early one evening when he was heading north on Clark Street. When he got to the light at Fullerton and Clark Streets, he was flagged down by a couple (a black woman and a white man). The woman was carrying two shopping bags. When Ifok stopped for them, the man kissed the woman, opened the door for her, shut it after she had sat down and told her he would see her at 10:00 PM.

"6000 N. Marine Drive, please," she said, bending over to look at Ifok's chauffeur license which was displayed on the dashboard.

"Okay" Ifok said, activating the meter while taking off.

"I like your name. Are you from the islands?" she asked.

"Which islands? Ifok asked.

"The West Indies" she said.

"No, I am from Africa" Ifok said.

"Wow, your accent is neat. Africans are nice people and I like them. But I have never had the opportunity to be intimately close to one," she said.

When the lady made that last statement Ifok reasoned that she either wanted a quickie or a sexual relationship. Ifok was ready for either option but he decided to play it cool and get her phone number and call her later for a date. At the end of the ride, the woman gave Ifok a $2 tip and asked him to help her carry her bags to her apartment. Ifok parked his cab and got hold of the passenger's bag, but as they walked past the doorman of her building he gave them a look which Ifok would never forget. It was the type of look you would give to someone you did not want to have anything to do with.

When they arrived at her apartment, the lady asked Ifok to sit down and offered him a glass of wine. She came and sat by him on the sofa and Ifok held her breasts and kissed her several times but anytime he tried to caress her genital area, she pushed his hand away. Later, she got up and told Ifok she had a surprise for him.

"I am not a woman. I am a man," she/he said, using a special lock to secure the door of the apartment on the inside. Ifok just looked at her/him like a silly sheep would. He had been had. He was virtually a prisoner of this woman/man.

"Why didn't you tell me that earlier? I would have left just after bringing your bags upstairs. Anyway, open the door and let me out," Ifok pleaded.

No. There is no way I am going to let you go now. You will have to make love to me first. I have heard you Africans are good lovers and I feel fortunate to have you here with me," she/he said.

"No way. I cannot make love to you. I will die if I do that. It is against the customs of my tribe," Ifok said, walking to the window and thinking of possible escape routes. Her/his apartment was on the tenth floor and that ruled out an escape through a window.

"Forget about the customs of your tribe in Africa. You are in America now. I will never let you leave till you make love to me," she/he said.

Ifok did not respond to the last statement. He just sat there, staring into space and quietly thinking about how to secure his release. Sex with her/him was out, because she/he would have to kill him first to get to that. After keeping quiet for about thirty minutes, Ifok started begging this person to set him free.

"I cannot make love to you because I have never done that before and I do not intend to start that now. You look like a nice person and there are people in this city who will be too glad to jump into bed with you. So, why force me? There is nothing special about Africans as far as sex is concerned. I know an African who is a homosexual. His name is Recko. If you will give me your number I will give it to him and he will call you so that the two of you can get together," Ifok said. He could see from the expression on her/his face that he was making progress.

"Let me go, please. That way we can be good friends," Ifok concluded.

She/he wrote her/his phone number on a piece of paper, gave it to Ifok and let him out. When he got to the main entrance of the building, the doorman turned his head as soon as his eyes met Ifok's. If he only knew what Ifok had gone through he would have felt sorry for him. Ifok threw away the phone number as soon as he got out of the building. When he got into his cab, he sat behind the steering wheel for about thirty minutes, just staring into space and thinking about all the terrible things that could have happened to him during his "imprisonment." When he started his cab he said to himself loudly: "One needs to be very careful in this country. There are too many deranged and dangerous people on the loose. In Africa, she/he would have been still in the closet, and would not have been out there trapping people into dalliances; she/he would have been beaten up by the public. No more quickies and one-night stands for me" He drove straight home and went to bed after drinking about half a pint of whiskey to calm his nerves.

Ifok was so shaken up by this incident that for sometime he suspected most of the women he met were men. To retain his sanity, to told his closest friends about his experience; he just could not keep what had happened to himself.

About a month later, he was surprised by another male passenger who offered to give him oral sex. He had picked up this well-dressed on the Magnificent Mile of North Michigan Avenue, who had stated he was going to an address in the 6100 block of North Sheridan Road, a very nice area. As soon as the cab took off, Ifok thought he heard his passenger mumble something in a very soft voice. Ifok did not respond because he did not understand what the man said, and he had a strange look on his face when Ifok had eye contact with him in the rearview mirror. After a few minutes, the passenger said softly, "Driver, I want to suck your dick." Ifok pretended he did not hear what the man had said. Evidently, his non-response angered the passenger who stated in a loud voice, "Hey cabbie, I said I want to suck your dick." Ifok replied in an equally loud voice, "Cut the shit out. You are not sucking any dick in my cab." After that exchange, the passenger did not utter a word till the end of the trip. He thanked Ifok and gave him a good tip.

"There are as many strange characters in the downtown area as the south side." Ifok said to himself. Bizarre episodes are still part of a cabbie's job!

Meanwhile, Ifok's marriage was falling apart. Zenny worked during the day and went to school at night. After two semesters, Ifok felt he was entitled to know her grades and how she was faring. She told Ifok she was not going to show him her grades because he did not pay her school fees. Two weeks later, she told Ifok she was going on a vacation to Jamaica.

"How are going to come by the money for this trip? Ifok asked.

"I have saved about $300, and I expect you to help out with the remaining $100," Zenny said.

"You must be losing your mind to expect some money from me for this trip. All you have in the bank is $300 and you are going to use that for a trip to Jamaica. Maybe that makes sense to you but it does not to me. Anyway, I will suggest you give some thought to the concept of marriage while on this trip," Ifok said.

"I am going on this trip. Nothing you say is going to stop me," Zenny concluded.

After this conversation, Zenny and Ifok never talked about this trip until the day of Zenny's departure. On that day, Ifok refused to drive her to the airport; she took a cab. Because the kids went to stay with their grandmother, Ifok lived alone during his wife's trip. This offered him the opportunity to think seriously of his marriage. He concluded that he would be better off living alone. To come by the money to move to his own apartment, he decided to stay on the road longer and make more money. He opened a special savings account into which he planned to deposit $50 every week. By the time Zenny returned from her trip, Ifok had cooled down enough to make the decision to not discuss separation with Zenny till he had saved enough money—about $600.

CHAPTER 7

Good Vibrations

One weekend in January, 1980, Ifok saw an advertisement in the Chicago Tribune for which he submitted his resume. It was for a director of development for a social service organization and the qualifications required were a master's degree and, at least, three years of experience in community development. Three weeks after submitting his resume, Ifok was invited for an interview. At this interview, the executive director of the organization asked Ifok to write a ten-page paper about the problems of the service area of the agency and suggest solutions for these problems. He was to submit this report in three weeks. He felt very good about this because, for once, American society was allowing him to make use of his six years of college education.

Ifok was conversant with the service area of this organization because that was where he lived before he went to Charleston in the Fall of 1977. His report covered the social, economic and physical problems of

this area and made recommendations for solving these problems; he submitted it within two weeks. When a month passed without a call or letter from the executive director, Ifok gave up any hope of being hired by that organization. He felt he had been used.

About six weeks after Ifok submitted his report, he received a letter from the executive director stating that a more qualified applicant had been hired for the position of director of development, but there was a position of counselor in one the organization's centers which he could apply for. He immediately went to the organization's main office and applied for that position. He was interviewed and hired by the executive director at a salary of $14,000 a year and given his letter of appointment to take to the center which was located in the public housing projects. He drove his cab to this site and was with the director for not more than thirty minutes. By the time he returned to his cab, someone had broken into it and stolen his CB radio. What a welcome to the neighborhood!

When Ifok informed his friends of his good fortune in obtaining that job, they were mostly skeptical because of the location of the worksite. One of them, Suuta, was very blunt.

"I will never work in the public housing project for $100,000 a year," Suuta said.

"The people there are low class, most of them are on public assistance, and have criminal records. When driving, I avoid State, Federal and Dearborn Streets between 31st and Garfield, where the projects are located. It is common knowledge that even the police are afraid to go there sometimes," Suuta continued

"I believe some of the people I pick in my cab are not that different from those in the projects. I am sure when the residents realize that you are there to help them and not take the little they have they will not harm you," Ifok said.

"You are very positive. This is the concrete jungle that Bob Marley has a song about. In Africa, only hunters go into the jungle to hunt game. Ordinary citizens are smart enough to not go there. You did not go into the jungle in Africa, why do you want to risk that here?" Suuta asked.

"Suuta, the housing project is not that dangerous. The people who live there are just poor and have little to look up to. I hope to be a positive influence and help them. You know, in the book, The Prince, Nicolo Machiavelli recommended that to survive, the ruler of a new kingdom should leave the residents' properties and their women alone and he would not have any problems governing. That will be my approach in this job at the projects," Ifok concluded.

The director of the center gave Ifok a medical report which had to be filled out by his doctor before he could start work. Because he did not have a personal physician, he went to the Board of Health clinic near his house. The medical examination indicated that Ifok had Hypertension. He was not surprised by that diagnosis because he had not been feeling well of late. He was given medication and advised to report to the clinic once a month.

On Ifok's first day on the job, the director of the center, Ms Hogan, took him round the center and introduced him to the other members of staff, sixteen in all. After this, they went to her office for a discussion of Ifok's responsibilities.

"You will be mainly responsible for the processing and maintenance of Title XX," she stated, handing him the government's Title XX manual. "Read this manual thoroughly. It specifies all the conditions and requirements of Title XX applications. You will also be a resource person for the parents of this center, and be responsible for recruitment of families. If you are scared to go to the public housing projects alone, I will have a member of staff accompany you," she continued.

"Okay, thank you," Ifok said.

Title XX was a federal government program which provided child care services for low income families while the parents were in school or working.

"Anyway, who told you about this position?" Ms Hogan asked.

"Well, I sent my resume to central office in response to an advertisement for a director of development. I was not hired for that position and the executive director wrote to inform me of this position," Ifok replied.

The executive director had hired Africans for the director of development position and two others, accountant and social worker, in the central office of the agency. Like Ifok, they were all very well qualified and from the west coast of Africa, where most of the ancestors of African Americans originated from.

"And what is your salary?" she asked.

"$14,000" Ifok said.

"That's nice. I just got an eleven percent raise," she said.

The question about his income bothered Ifok, and he did not like the look on Ms Hogan's face when he told her how much he would be making; additionally, he felt she did not have to tell him of her recent salary increase. Whatever was on Ms Hogan's mind, he would know with the passage of time.

Two weeks after he started working as a counselor, an incident occurred that convinced Ifok he would be better off living alone. Pappy, an African friend of Ifok's who lived about half a block away called Ifok one Friday night, around 9:30 PM and asked him to come to his apartment for a drink. Ifok told him he would come but not drink because of his hypertension. Zenny, as usual, had gone to school that night. Ifok stayed at Pappy's for about three hours during which their conversation centered on problems encountered by foreigners. He left Pappy's house at about 1:00 AM and when he got to the front of his building he saw his wife getting out of another man's car. He waited for her and they entered their building together.

"Thank you very much, Zenny. I suspected something like this was going on all the time. Now I have proof. I cannot stay married to you any longer, and I shall start looking for an apartment tomorrow and move out in two weeks," Ifok said. Under normal circumstances Ifok would have hit her but he did not because Zenny had a loaded pistol in the apartment.

"That man just gave me a ride home, that's all. I met him at this party and since he was going my way, he decided to give me a ride," she said.

"I thought you went to school," Ifok said.

"Well, I went to school first and then on to the party," she replied.

"A wife indeed!" Ifok exclaimed. The phone rang.

"It's your friend. He wants to know if you are still alive. Pick up the phone and tell him he can move in with you in two weeks. Tell him the African fool has figured everything out," Ifok said.

Zenny picked up the phone, said "Yes" and "Bye" and hung up.

A week later Ifok found an apartment he liked, paid a security deposit and the manager informed him if everything he had stated on his application was true he could move in in two weeks. Zenny did not go out at all the following week; her classes ended all of a sudden. Ifok moved to his new apartment as planned. Zenny helped him pack his things on the day of his departure. He told her he would be in touch.

As counselor, Ifok was to organize the monthly meetings of the parent group. At these meetings suggestions were made, complaints aired and valuable information passed out. At his first meeting with the parent group, Ifok gave a very brief speech.

"Good morning, ladies. My name is Ifok Hasnem and I am your new counselor. My hours of work are from 9:00 AM to 5:00 PM and you should feel free to come and see me about any question or issue during these hours. I also have a list of schools and training programs you can enroll in. I hope to have a nice working relationship with each one of you, "Ifok said.

As soon as he was through giving his introductory speech, Ms Hogan got up and made the following remarks: "As you are all aware, I am the director of this center and I intend to be director every day. Anytime you have a question or problem you should let me know immediately. If I am not in, leave a message with my secretary and I will get in contact with you as soon as possible," she said. Some of the parents laughed as soon as Ms Hogan was through making these remarks. Ifok was confused because he felt his job description required the parents to bring all issues to him and then he would provide guidance; some issues he would have to discuss with the center director. He decided to go by what he considered proper procedure. This was to notify Ms Hogan of his contacts with the parents and details relating to their participation in the program; Ms Hogan could do whatever she liked with the reports of parents who went directly to her.

This agency which hired Ifok had a uniform code. All staff members had to wear an African smock or dashiki over their clothes when on agency sites or at agency functions. Most of the staff did not like wearing this uniform, neither did Ifok. They, however, thought Ifok being an African would be used to that style of dressing up. They were surprised to learn Ifok had never worn a smock or dashiki in this country till he was hired by the agency.

The agency had an Afrocentric curriculum for the children. Ifok learned the executive director, Mr Jones, had done some research in an East African country years ago and was impressed by the implementation of principles similar to Kwanzaa there. Kwanzaa was originated by Dr Maulana Karenga, a professor at California State University in Long Beach, California in 1966, to honor the customs and history of African Americans. Its seven principles are meant to remind African Americans of their past, prepare them for the present, and equip them with skills for the future. The children enjoyed participating in the rituals of Kwanzaa.

After a while it became obvious to Ifok that Mr Jones was aware of the negative views of some staff about the direction of the agency, but he was intent on inculcating in poor black families the spirit of community, cooperation and hard work, all areas covered by Kwanzaa. Mr Jones was bent on encouraging young African-Americans to utilize the program to get careers, get off of Welfare, and to be better able to take care of their families; this was to be done at the same time as the children were being educated about their ancestry and history. Ifok believed in that aspect of Mr Jones' vision but also understood the ambivalence of some staff who made occasional unflattering comments about Africa to his (Ifok's) hearing. Ifok worked hard to get along with the staff and parents of his center; he tried to get on everyone's good side, even those he did not care much for.

Kwanzaa was foreign to Ifok who was from the west coast of Africa and had lived in the city most of his life. Ifok reasoned Kwanza could be applicable in some form in the smaller towns and villages of West Africa, but not in the big cities where some people were copying, blindly or not, the Western way of life, and robberies, official corruption, drug dealing, auto theft and scams were becoming common in the 1980s; some of the brothers and sisters in the cities of West Africa had been watching too many Western movies, he surmised.

Ifok's work involved sending a lot of correspondence, mainly notices, to parents. During the first three weeks, anytime he wanted to send a notice to parents he would prepare the draft, give it to the typist for typing after which he xeroxed it and sent copies to the parents with a copy to Ms Hogan. After the first three weeks, Ms Hogan informed Ifok she had to approve all notices to parents. When Ifok submitted a draft of his next correspondence for her approval, Ms Hogan added her name and title to the bottom and the letter was sent out with Ifok's signature and hers on it. On a number of occasions, Ms Hogan made additions to Ifok's draft, usually in the form of paragraphs and these always contained severe grammatical errors and spelling mistakes. Nevertheless, Ifok signed those letters; he did not know how to correct his supervisor without offending her. One day, however, the mistakes in Ms Hogan's addition were so serious that Ifok refused to sign it. Ms Hogan wanted to know why.

"Why didn't you sign the letter?" Ms Hogan asked.

"I did not sign it because I do not approve of its composition," Ifok replied.

"What is wrong with it? I consider your refusal to sign it an act of insubordination," Ms Hogan said.

"You can call it whatever you want. There are too many grammatical errors in it. I will sign any letter if I agree with its content and composition. This letter is not well-written and I will not sign it," Ifok said. The letter was sent out with only Ms Hogan's signature on it.

Around this time, some staff members who were friendly with Ifok told him of statements Ms Hogan had made about him: Ms Hogan did not like him because she felt he had been earmarked to replace her. On one of the few occasions they had friendly chats, Ms Hogan frankly told Ifok how she felt.

"You know, I did not want you to be hired as counselor," she said.

"Why?" Ifok asked.

"Frankly, I think you are overqualified for the position. Additionally, I do not trust Mr Jones, the executive director. I think he intentionally brought you here so that you will take up my position after he gets rid of me," she said.

"Well, I do not know the plans of Mr Jones but I know mine. I will not accept a center director's position in this organization, so you do not have to worry about me. I have started sending my resume out and I am hoping for a positive response one of these days," Ifok said.

"With your qualifications and willingness to work, you will find a good position soon," she said.

Despite what Ifok told Ms Hogan, it appeared she was still insecure in her position and this drove her to do many things to make Ifok uncomfortable at this job. Through the grapevine at the center, Ifok heard of everything she said about him.

As part of his responsibilities as a counselor, Ifok maintained contact with schools and training institutions and referred the parents to them, as requested, and for compliance with Title XX regulations. Some of the parents did not have high school diplomas, thus limiting their training potential. There were, however, a number of schools claiming to provide training for office work for those without high school diplomas or GED (General Education Diploma). Ifok wondered how persons with such qualifications could be hired in an office environment. He realized that some parents had been providing documentation from such institutions to comply with the program, but not getting the promised training; and some were not going to school despite the provision of such documentation.

Ifok felt it was his responsibility to ensure the parents acquired marketable skills to help them get off public assistance. He encouraged those without high school diplomas to register for GED classes and he obtained information from Loop College in Downtown Chicago about available non-degree and certificate programs. He set up a system for monitoring attendance at some schools. He called a meeting of the parents, with the center director in attendance, and announced that submission of bogus documentation would be reported to Central Office. Three of the 105 parents of the center took their children out of the program after Ifok's action; 2 of them returned after about 3 months, claiming their children missed their classmates and the program; and the third kept her child home when she became pregnant again.

During the month of June, 1982, Ms Hogan went on her annual three-week vacation and Ms Drag, a teacher, was designated to be in charge of the center during Ms Hogan's absence. By this time, Ifok had become so frustrated working at this center that he was ready to settle for a part-time job and quit this one.

One afternoon, Ifok was talking to Ms Drag when she brought up the issue of additional duties assigned by

Ms Hogan. These extra duties included going to the store to purchase items for the center, and waiting at the center till all the children were picked up at the end of each day, all tasks performed by other staff and teachers in other centers of the organization. Ifok told her he was not going to perform those duties anymore because he was not hired as a messenger or security guard. Ms Drag called Ms Hogan and told her everything Ifok had said. Ms Hogan called Ifok at the center the next day and told him she would like to have a conference with him when she returned to work.

They had their conference as planned, and this time Ifok was brutally honest.

"I have been told you have decided not to perform the additional duties I assigned you recently," she said.

"Yes, I was hired as a counselor, and not as a messenger or security guard. Other counselors in this organization do not perform such duties. Why should I? Show me where they are specified on my job description. I have enough work to keep me busy," Ifok said.

"I will suggest that you resign from your position If you are not willing to carry out genuine orders from me," she said.

"Well, you are my supervisor and I will let you know when I make the decision to resign," Ifok said.

Two weeks later Ifok resigned from his job as counselor. In his letter of resignation to the executive director, he stated that the harassment perpetuated by Ms Hogan was responsible for his decision to leave. Ms Hogan finally got her wish.

CHAPTER 8

Same Old,
Same Old/ Chasing
The Dollar

A month after he resigned from his job as a counselor, Ifok started dating Joyce, a 27 year old black woman. She lived in the projects with her three kids and had known Ifok only casually. They met at The Swinging Omen, a reggae club on the north side of the city. This club always had an international "flavor" because it was frequented by immigrants and Americans who had had the opportunity to live outside the United States in the past; the environment was always very friendly. Ifok's friend, Noon, worked as the manager on some nights and on such nights, Ifok did not have to pay the admission fee; on some nights, he got free drinks too.

"What are you doing in my club? Joyce asked when she saw him at the club.

"What are you doing in my neighborhood?" Ifok also asked her.

"Well, a friend of mine introduced me to this joint about a year ago and I have been coming here occasionally since then. Someone told me you do not work at the center anymore," she continued.

"I resigned about a month ago," Ifok said.

"I don't blame you. It is very difficult working with some of our people in the projects. I know that because I have lived there all my life. You have found a better job, I suppose" she said.

"No, not yet. It's still a jungle out there," Ifok said. "I will give you my number so that you can call me sometime. I am also job hunting. I lost my job two months ago," Joyce said.

They exchanged phone numbers. Ifok bought her a drink and they danced till the club closed at 2:00 AM. Because Joyce was with two of her girlfriends, Ifok did not make any moves likely to discourage Joyce from wanting to see him again. He was very formal.

Joyce called Ifok three days after their meeting. Her children had left for school and she was at home watching television. Ifok did not want to take a chance and go to her place. He told her he would be cooking something African and special for lunch and invited her to come over. To Ifok's surprise, Joyce accepted the invitation. He was to pick her up in front of her building at 11.30 AM.

Joyce was not much of a drinking person and drank just a shot of vodka. Ifok, on the other hand, had about three shots. They had sex before the food got ready and then jumped into bed again after eating. Ifok considered himself very lucky because he had not had sex in more than a month. Unsure of how long the liaison would last, he got as much as his stamina would allow.

"You are a good lover," Joyce told Ifok while they were lying in bed.

"Come on, you are kidding. I am told smart women tell men that to keep them in line. It makes us feel good about ourselves. Every man wants to be considered the best in that department. Thanks for the compliment, anyway," Ifok said.

"I really mean it. You are a good lover," she said.

"You are a good lover too. You have the most shapely figure I have encountered. You are slender with the right curves. I hope we will continue to see each other," Ifok said.

"You know why I like you? You have a way of massaging my ego that makes me feel good about myself. Things you do and say, and the way you express them turn me on," Joyce said

"You have a nice personality to match your looks," Ifok said, pulling her closer and kissing her.

"Hey! You can have me anytime" Joyce said.

"That's good to know" Ifok said.

After this session, Joyce and Ifok got together about three times each week. Joyce had a boyfriend, Albert, who was at her house at weekday nights and on weekends. Her encounters with Ifok took place during the day and at Ifok's apartment. One day she dropped a bombshell on Ifok.

"You know I like women too and I feel you should know," she said.

"Wow! So you like both men and women, separately or together? Ifok asked.

"I am bisexual but of late I tend to enjoy sex more with a woman than a man," Joyce said.

Ifok did not say anything. He just laid there while Joyce went to sleep. Joyce was his first experience with an admitted bisexual woman. When she woke up two hours later, Ifok was still wide awake, thinking.

"Are you really bisexual? Ifok asked.

"Yes. I will introduce my female lover to you sometime. She is called Sheila. She is very attractive and I love her," Joyce said.

After this, no mention was made of Joyce's bisexuality until a month later when Joyce called to say she wanted Ifok to meet Sheila. Joyce and Sheila went to Ifok's apartment at the scheduled time. First, Ifok started having sex with Joyce while Sheila watched; she later joined them, kissing Joyce while caressing her own breasts. After this, Ifok watched them make love to each other; during the course of this event they both started moaning and groaning, and Ifok became sexually aroused again. When they were done, Ifok made love to Sheila with Joyce's permission. They had two more threesomes before Joyce and Sheila broke up their relationship.

On another occasion, Joyce revealed more of her personal life experiences which shocked Ifok. They were watching television and during a break there was a preview of a documentary on incest, scheduled for showing the following week.

"I have to watch this movie" she said softly.

"Why is it important for you to watch this movie?" Ifok asked. When he looked at her there were tears in her eyes.

"My father slept with me and my older sister for years. I am angry now because he has started sleeping with our youngest sister, Ruth. Our mother is an alcoholic and our father gives her alcohol till she passes out every night, giving him the opportunity to spend the night with our sister. He did the same thing to my sister and I when we lived with them," Joyce said, shedding more tears.

Joyce's father started having sex with her from age 12 to age 20, when she moved out. He fathered her first child, Motta. Her older sister's second child, Edith, was also fathered by this man. Ifok felt something had to be done to stop this monster. He advised Joyce to make a report to the police. She said she would not know how to start her story. The documentary on incest was shown as scheduled. Joyce invited her sisters to her house where they watched it. They held each other closely and cried throughout the show. They called the Incest Hotline advertised after the show and reported their father.

Officials of the State of Illinois agency responsible for child abuse took up the case and a report was made to the police. Joyce's father was charged with sexually abusing his teenaged daughter and taken to court. The family later decided to withdraw the case. The State reduced the charges and Joyce's father was placed on probation and received court-ordered counseling. Joyce's aunt was given custody of Ruth. A few months later, Joyce got a job as a receptionist at a manufacturing company. Her schedule left her with very little time for more sexual encounters with Ifok. They ceased to be lovers and became friends, contacting each other occasionally by phone.

On the advice of a lady he had met at a friend's party, Ifok decided to apply for State of Illinois positions. With his background in the social sciences and experience in the government and non-profit sectors, his new friend argued, that was what he should do. This friend also suggested that Ifok should elect to work outside Chicago since positions in other parts of the State would be easier to get. For a period of time, Ifok visited the State of Illinois personnel office in Downtown Chicago where jobs were regularly posted.

Despite his friend's advice, Ifok only looked for positions open in Chicago, which were plentiful. There were ratings for job applicants based on their qualifications. These were as follows: A – Highly Qualified; B – Well Qualified; C – Qualified; and D – Not Qualified. According to instructions stated on each job announcement, those with high qualifications were considered for interview first, and ratings lasted for a year. In all, Ifok applied for 12 positions, of which he was rated as highly qualified for eleven and well qualified for one. When he received a letter for an interview, it was for the twelfth one with a rating of well qualified.

Despite Ifok's initial disappointment about the interview request, he was happy because he knew if selected his life would change for the better. The interview was for the position of Methods and Procedures Advisor with the Department of Mental Health and Developmental Disabilities, and the qualifications required were a bachelor's degree and a year's experience in program compliance. Ifok was interviewed by a panel of three women. One read the job description and asked him to state his qualifications for the job.

"I was trained for public service by the government of my home country, and I worked as a civil servant for a number of years before my immigration to this country. Since coming here, I have acquired a number of degrees and been employed by a non-profit in a program compliance role," Ifok said.

"You are very qualified, that's why you have been invited to this interview," a panel member stated. "The concern we have is this. This position is monotonous work, requiring visits to facilities and homes which have signed contracts with the State. We wonder if someone with your qualifications will be satisfied with this position," she concluded.

"I like program compliance. This is the area of my interest and experience. It has been a long journey to this interview, having also been employed as cab driver and security guard, and as counselor in the housing projects in the past. I am humble and work well with others. I believe my background has prepared me well to handle the responsibilities of a Methods and Procedures Advisor, and I hope to have the opportunity to do so," Ifok concluded. Impressive presentation by Ifok. He was told there were three more candidates to be interviewed, after which a selection would be made. He was not hired for the position.

PROGRAM
ANALYST

About a year after resigning from his position of counselor, Ifok saw a blind advertisement in the local paper for a program analyst position. He submitted his resume and he was scheduled for an interview at the non-profit agency which had placed the advertisement. The interview went very well, and the interviewer, the director of programs, claimed to have read about current events in Ifok's country in the Christian Science Monitor. Ifok was hired for this position. It was in the heart of downtown, and professional attire was required. Occasionally, some of his friends saw him in the downtown area, dressed up for work. That gave him a nice feeling about himself because the years of hard work had paid off. He liked this job very much because it required usage of his planning and program compliance training and experience. His agency had government contracts which required allocation and monitoring of funds to other agencies for community development projects. His responsibilities included investigation of socio-economic issues of interest to management in its decision-making, and provision of technical assistance to agencies.

Provision of technical assistance proved to be very interesting. The agencies which needed such help most of the time were the smaller ones with little of no management controls or expertise to ensure compliance with program requirements. Some pastors and deacons of very small churches fell into this category. Any social service agency or group with a board of directors which identified community needs in their service areas was eligible. Helping some of these agencies account for services provided was an ordeal Ifok wished he did not have to go through. One pastor of a small storefront church confessed to Ifok that he used the allocated funds to buy food for his congregation and family members; and he begged Ifok to write off the amount. After Ifok insisted he still had to provide documentation on how the funds were spent, the pastor went underground. The agency decided to not pursue this pastor because the amount involved was so small.

Despite Ifok's help, 5 small agencies and church-affiliated groups were de-linked because of non-compliance with program rules. With time, Ifok's agency amended its policies to enable it to provide most of the funding to bigger non-profits and companies depending on the services. The rationale was that they already had the organizational set-up and structure and the general public was aware of their existence and activities. The smaller agencies did not like that, but public funds had to be allocated judiciously.

One Sunday morning, Ifok was driving home after buying groceries from one of the convenient stores on Argyle Street, between Sheridan Road and Broadway. He was going west on Argyle toward Broadway when the traffic light turned red. Directly ahead of him was a police car with two police officers and an individual. The gestures or movement Ifok observed did not suggest a friendly interaction in the police car. When the light turned green, the police car did not move for about thirty seconds and Ifok could not drive around them because of the traffic going in the other direction (East). After Ifok honked to alert them they had the green light, one of the policemen got out of the police car and came to Ifok's window.

"Why did you honk?" the policeman asked Ifok.

"I honked to alert you guys that you got the green light," Ifok replied.

"You fucking Jamaican. Go back to your country," the policeman said, on hearing Ifok's accent.

"You are a stupid man, officer. How can you serve and protect me, with your prejudice?" Ifok asked, pointing at the phrase "We Serve and Protect" boldly printed on the police car.

"I have some American Indian friends in Chippewa Falls, Wisconsin. They think after I leave for my country, you should also move to wherever your ancestors came from," Ifok concluded.

After this exchange, Ifok got the opportunity to drive around this police car. He turned right on Broadway and was almost at Foster Avenue when he saw the flashing light behind him in his rearview mirror. He stopped his car. It was the same police officer.

"What is the problem, officer," Ifok asked.

"May I see your driver's license and insurance," the officer asked.

Ifok, who was driving on a ticket, produced the ticket and his proof of insurance.

"Do you know your license plate has expired?" he asked Ifok.

"Yes, but I mailed in the license renewal form and the required payment before it expired last week, and I am expecting the sticker anytime soon." Ifok replied. He did not have that proof with him, though.

"I have to take you to the station. You post bail and get a court date to tell your story to the judge," the policeman said. The policeman was determined to lock him up, and he did.

Ifok was advised to park his car properly by the side of the street. He was locked up in the back seat area of the police car with its barriers and driven to the station on Foster near Damen, a distance of about a mile. At the station, he did not have the $35 fee for posting bail, so he was locked up for seven hours till a friend came to bail him out. He was given a court date but was freed by the judge when the policeman did not show up. Ifok developed a strong hatred for Chicago Police Department after his encounter with this policeman, who managed to put him behind bars for the first time in America.

When Ifok discussed the issue about his arrest and court date with Mr Glass, his immediate supervisor who was also an attorney, he (Mr Glass) advised him to file a formal complaint with the Internal Affairs Division (IAD) of the Chicago Police Department. Mr Glass said there had been many cases on record of policemen arresting people, mainly black men for the flimsiest of offences, booking them for court, and then not showing up to present their cases to judges for adjudication. He offered to help Ifok if he had an appointment with the IAD, but Ifok decided to not take the issue any further.

In early July, 1989, Ifok took a two-week personal leave from his job, during which he visited a friend in Milwaukee, Wisconsin. His company was preparing to move from the downtown area to a less built-up area, about half a mile away on the near northside. On his return to work, it was a regular workday till around 3.00 PM when he got a call from the president of the agency.

"Hello, Ifok. Can you come to my office right now?" Mr Trat, the president asked.

"Yes Sir. I will be right there," Ifok responded. The president had never called him before so Ifok suspected something was wrong. When Ifok got to Mr Trat's office, Mr Trat was sitting at his desk with a pile of about twenty files to his left. He picked one, which was evidently Ifok's.

"How was your vacation?" he asked Ifok.

"It was nice. I visited a friend in Milwaukee," Ifok replied.

"Welcome back, Ifok. This agency is going through a re-organization which will affect all departments.

Some departments will become smaller while others become bigger. We have decided to eliminate two positions, including yours, in your department. You will receive three months pay as severance and have the opportunity to apply for any newly-created or available positions of interest to you. You will also be eligible for unemployment benefits for a period of six months. Mr Glass will answer any questions you may have," Mr Trat concluded.

"Thank you, Sir," Ifok said, shaking Mr Trat's hand. He returned to his office and gave the bad news to his co-workers. He had to leave the building immediately in order not to be escorted out, as had been done to others in the past. Winnie, the staff assistant of his department promised to mail him any personal items he could not take home that day. That was the end of the best job he had had in America to date. Based on his experience, he knew getting another decent job was not going to be easy. Mentally, he was not ready to settle for any job, just to pay his bills, as he had done in the past. He decided to return to his home country.

Ifok called his parents around 2.00 PM Chicago time, which was 8.00 PM in Africa. His mother, Adeye, who picked up the phone expressed surprise since Ifok had not called in months; she had become used to the infrequency of his calls.

"Mom, I am coming home," Ifok said.

"Thank you, Jesus!" exclaimed Adeye. "Are you coming to visit or to stay for good? She asked.

"For good," Ifok replied.

"There is no better place to live than in your own country. America is a nice place where one can make a lot of money, but it is also a very dangerous place and there is a lot of discrimination against blacks and foreigners, based on what I have been reading. You qualify on both fronts being a black foreigner," Adeye said.

"Yes, there is a lot of discrimination in America, just like in Africa where some tribes still discriminate against others," Ifok said.

"Talk to your daddy," Adeye said, handing the phone to Kobi.

"Hello, my son," Kobi started. "I overheard your conversation with your mother. I am very happy to learn you have decided to come home. There were times when I worried about you and wondered why you have decided to stay in a foreign land for many years of your most productive life. As a former civil servant in good standing, you could be hired for a higher position based on your qualifications," Kobi said.

"That's what I am working on now," Ifok said.

"Thank you very much for not bringing disgrace to this family. Of late, stories of the imprisonment of some of your compatriots in the United States for drug dealing have been published in the local newspapers, thus humiliating their families. People returning home with a lot of money are suspected to have been drug dealers in the United States. You know, I always believed that you would never stoop that low to make money. I am so proud of you," Kobi concluded.

"Thank you very much, Dad, for believing in my judgment. I will provide details of the plan for my return home later," Ifok concluded.

CHAPTER 9

Return To Home Country

After the phone conversation with his parents, the die was cast and Ifok was going home, with or without a job offer, after living in the United States for about 16 years. If he did not get a job offer before his departure, he would apply for re-instatement in the Civil Service based on his qualifications, after his arrival there.

"Going back to school was the easy part," he said. "It's getting a good, decent job which is very difficult. Those of us who left our parents and other relatives with influence home, are in serious trouble. To get a good job and keep it, you must know a politician or someone with clout. By good job, I mean a job which matches your qualifications, pays a decent salary, and has room for advancement. Also, if you are hired for a job without a recommendation by someone of influence, you could lose it anytime," he concluded.

In preparation for his return home, Ifok contacted the embassy of his country for a list of available government jobs. He had fantasized about finding an available position in the embassy in Washington DC. But no, such positions were always given to his countrymen with clout. He was given the requisite application which he filled out and was scheduled for an interview in a month.

Ifok found the interview very interesting. The embassy official who interviewed him, Mr Modah, was very nice and polite.

"I see that you have been in the United States for a long time. Our country needs people like you to inject fresh ideas in her development plans," he said. "Anyway, are you related to Mr Hasnem, the attorney?" Mr Modah asked.

"Yes, he is my brother but we have not been corresponding for years," Ifok said.

"He defended some friends of mine in a very high profile case before the High Court over ten years ago. He did an excellent job," Mr Modah continued.

"That's nice to hear. I will tell him of your kind words when I go home," Ifok said.

"Have you ever been home to visit since you came to this country?" Mr Modah asked.

"No. My country is my country. I do not think I have to visit to check things out before going back finally. My country is the only one that I have," Ifok said.

"I admire your patroitism or nationalism, whichever is applicable in this instance. Our country needs more people with such ideas," Mr Mudah said.

"You see, I never always had such ideas. There was a time when I never had such ideas and wanted to live in this country for as long as possible. I guess I changed with age. I believe many African-Americans would go back home if they had the choice I have," Ifok said.

"Good. I believe you will be a good and hard working public servant. I will check your references and educational qualifications and send your particulars to the Public Service Commission back home for approval. Usually the commission acts on applications within 90 days," Mr Mudah said.

"Okay" Ifok said.

"If you are offered a job, how soon would you be ready to start?" Mr Mudah asked.

"90 days after notification," Ifok said immediately.

"I will suggest you take 180 days which would give you enough time to ship your personal belongings and have some rest before you start work. Good luck. I will get in contact with you as soon as the Public Service Commission notifies me of its decision," Mr Mudah stated, rising from his chair and shaking Ifok's hand.

"Thank you" Ifok said

ASSISTANT SECRETARY, MINISTRY OF ECONOMIC PLANNING

Ifok and his African friends, most of whom had lived in this country for more than 10 years, had talked about leaving this pressure cooker called America, but none of them acted on this issue like Ifok had just done. To avoid unnecessary arguments, he kept his Washington DC interview secret. After he received his letter of appointment for the position of Assistant Secretary in the

Ministry of Economic Planning, he made arrangements for shipping his household items three weeks before his departure for Africa on a cold February morning in 1990. He had arranged a stopover in Amsterdam in the Netherlands for 5 days to purchase a Toyota Corolla at the weekly auto auction and had it shipped to Africa. Since he had been promised a government vehicle in his new job, he planned to register the Toyota as a taxi and hire a driver to make money for him on the side. Instead of requiring the driver to pay before taking the cab out every day, as in Chicago, Ifok would allow the driver to make payment at the end of each work day. The government made arrangements with a shipping agent to take delivery of Ifok's household items and transport them to his assigned bungalow. Welcome back, Ifok!

Ifok's plane landed at the international airport of the capital city at 8.00 PM. As usual there were many people at the arrival gate to welcome friends and relatives returning home. The arrival lounge was hot and humid, and there were armed security personnel- police and military- all over the place. Although there was a big posted sign that only armed security and custom officials were allowed in that area, it was common to see men and women in civilian clothes hustling the passengers for tips. That frightened Ifok as he tried to identify his 5 suitcases on the carousel. He kept looking at the public gallery to see if he could see his elder brother, Naley, who had promised to pick him up. After a while, he gave up looking for his brother because there were hundreds of people in that gallery. After Ifok got his bags he was approached by a gentleman who introduced himself as an official of the Ministry of Economic Planning, the agency Ifok would be working for.

"Welcome home, Mr Ifok Hasnem, the official said, handing Ifok an envelope. "Please read the instructions carefully and call me within 72 hours so that you will be taken to your official residence. The items you shipped have already been delivered there. You will report for work exactly two weeks from today," the official concluded.

After that encounter, Ifok pulled the cart with his suitcases to one of the Customs booths for processing. He had been advised by a friend in Chicago to give the customs official a $5 tip to avoid being thoroughly searched which could take a long time. After going through Customs, Ifok pushed his cart to the arrival gate where his brother was waiting.

"Mom and Dad have decided to not go to bed tonight till I bring you home," Naley said. The ride to the house was fast, although a little a little bumpy because various sections of the route were in states of disrepair. Ifok was surprised by what little changes had been made. When they got to the family compound, the night watchman opened the gate and Naley drove to the entrance of the main building where their 88 year old father stood with open arms to welcome his youngest son home. Ifok's 79 year old mother could not stay awake till his arrival.

The next day, Ifok did not go out. He spent time with his Mom and Dad, and two brothers and sister who also stopped by. A special African ceremonial meal of pounded yam, palm oil and hard-boiled eggs was prepared for all members of the household. Kobi sprinkled some of the food at the entrance of the main building and called on Almighty God, as required by tradition, to bless all the residents of the house and drive away evil spirits.

"There is a question I want to ask you. I know your daddy does not like talking about the issue but I am sure it bothers him too," Adeye started. "Did you father any children in America?" she asked.

"No, I did not, but I was married for sometime to a woman with two children and we did not agree on having more children," Ifok replied.

"Do you have a problem having children?" Adeye asked.

"No, I do not have such a problem. In America, I always had a girlfriend but such relationships were mainly for companionship, not procreation," Ifok responded.

"Kobi, your son now thinks like an American. A 44-year old man with only one child, a child he had almost 20 years ago. That is strange. There is something wrong with you," Adeye continued.

"Mom, there is nothing wrong with me. I want to have more children but I have to meet someone interested in the same outcome," Ifok said.

"That's good to know. Anyway, I am glad you did not have children with an American, because I would not have had the opportunity to see or meet them. I have to get to work and find you a wife here," Adeye concluded.

"Mom, do not worry. I will do well on my own," Ifok said.

On the third day after his arrival home, Ifok decided to go look for his son, Rojo. His ex-wife, Gama, did not take their son to see Ifok's parents from time to time, as she had promised 16 years ago before returning home. She re-married soon after returning home and had three more children. Ifok obtained information about where Gama and her family lived and the school Rojo was attending.

Rojo was 18 years old and a high school senior. Their first meeting was at Rojo's school and it was short. Many people said Rojo looked like a younger Ifok and Ifok could see that, but there was also a striking resemblance to his mother when he smiled.

"I am Ifok, your father. I just returned home after years abroad," Ifok said, shaking Rojo's hand.

"Mom told me about you," Rojo replied.

"Right now, I am staying at my parents' home but I will be moving to my new government apartment tomorrow. My address will be 10 Tampe Avenue, Apartment 7B.

Stop by there anytime after tomorrow so that we can talk some more. I brought you some items. Say Hi to your mom and family," Ifok concluded .

"I will be there on Saturday," Rojo promised.

Rojo showed up at the promised time, and he and Ifok had a nice conversation.

"You were eighteen months old when I left for the United States," Ifok started.

"Why did you not take me with you?" Rojo asked.

"Your mother and I had planned that she would join me after about a year and you would follow two years later and start kindergarten there, but things did not work out as we had planned and we decided to go our separate ways," Ifok explained.

"What are your plans after your high school graduation?" Ifok asked.

"I plan to study Business Administration at the local university," Rojo replied.

"That's a good field," Ifok replied.

He gave Rojo the clothes he had brought him and they agreed to be in contact now that Ifok had come home permanently. Rojo stopped by on three more occasions to get money from Ifok. He never brought Ifok a copy of his school certificate results, as Ifok had requested. Later, Ifok learned Rojo had not done well in the final exam.

Ifok's responsibilities involved the monitoring of government grants to local governmental units. He supervised a staff of 20 development agents, each of whom was responsible for one of the 20 districts of the country. Development agents traveled throughout the country to ensure that local councils complied with governmental programs and regulations and that local construction projects were on schedule. He visited all the district offices during his first month in office and decided that some changes were necessary to make the system more efficient and development agents more accountable. This did not please a lot of people in his ministry who were satisfied with the status quo and felt he was trying to impose American standards which would not work in Africa.

District development agents had a lot of authority in their jurisdictions. They advertised contracts, accepted bids, and selected contractors to undertake projects. After selecting contractors, district development agents sent the relevant documents to the Assistant Secretary who authorized payment before commencement of projects. After such authorization, the development agents were expected to monitor projects until their completion. This system was rife with corruption and Ifok decided to make some changes. Some district development agents and their relatives and friends and corrupt contractors were enriching themselves at taxpayer expense. Shoddy and/or uncompleted projects were common.

Ifok initiated a secret investigation which revealed the following: in some cases the selected bids were actually submitted after the closing dates for submissions; some contractors submitted very low bids, knowing fully well that they would not be able to complete the projects with such funds; and some contractors were cutting corners in order to increase their profit margins.

Ifok suspected some high government officials were silent partners of contractors who won bids. An incident which highlighted the need for change was a three-storey classroom block which had been constructed by a contactor with "connections." The structure collapsed a week before the official opening by the Minister. One construction worker died and two others were hospitalized with serious injuries. An investigation by the Department of Public Works and the Civil Engineering Department of the local university revealed serious issues with short-changing of building specifications and utilization of low quality building materials. Because of the public outcry over this incident, the contractor was charged with misuse of public funds and endangering the public.

With the support of the Minister, Ifok introduced a new system that involved the submission of all bids to local boards which submitted recommendations to the Assistant Secretary. As one would expect, most of the district development agents did not like the new arrangement since it reduced their clout and authority.

After working as the Assistant Secretary for two years, Ifok was promoted to the rank of Secretary, which mainly involved policy formulation and representing the minister at some meetings. He also met and married Yaabo, a 30-year old lawyer who worked in the Attorney General's Department. He and his wife moved to a new home on the outskirts of town. Their house had all the modern amenities, including a swimming pool.

In early June, 1992, Ifok and some friends went on a visit to Edumaf during that village's annual festival. It was his first visit to that place since his return home. He did not go with his wife because he had not told her of his experience there years ago. He was interested in finding out how the place had changed and if some of the people he knew in the past still lived there. He found out that all the elders who participated in the resolution of the dispute years ago were dead. Ifok did not seek or meet Maa, neither did he meet anyone who remembered him as the first district development officer. The village had changed considerably: there was a new high school; the small clinic had been upgraded to a hospital; electricity was available to anyone who could afford it; there were more drinking spots, and a night club which operated on Friday and Saturday nights; and there were regular buses operating between the village and the capital city daily. Ifok returned to the capital city satisfied that he had achieved his goal of a better job on his return to his home country.

"I am on a roll. You should come and visit. I do not know what made me stay in the United States for so long. I should have come home earlier," Ifok wrote to his American friends. To his African friends in the United States, he wrote: "You are wasting your time by staying in America long after you have achieved the purpose of your journey, namely, to get an education. Come home and be part of the action. Your country needs you."

Early in the morning of October 5, 1992, Ifok was doing his regular exercises when he heard the following announcement on the radio: "Good morning, countrymen. I am General Boko of the Army. The Armed Forces in cooperation with the Police Department have overthrown the corrupt civilian government of President Mpata. All Members of Parliament, Ministers and other heads of government departments are to report to the nearest police stations immediately." There was a pause of about two minutes and then another announcement: "Good morning. I am General Boko of the Army. The Armed Forces in cooperation with the Police Department have overthrown the corrupt civilian government of President Mpata. President Mpata is under house arrest. All Members of Parliament, Ministers and Secretaries of Ministries are to report to the nearest police stations for their own safety. The public is advised to remain calm and stay indoors. All acts of hooliganism and vandalism will be severely repressed. Further announcements will be made as necessary."

Ifok stopped exercising immediately and sat on the chair closest to the radio, staring at the wall in a daze. The announcement was followed immediately by the playing of military music. Yaabo was still asleep and unaware of what was happening. After about five minutes, Ifok got up, talking to himself as he walked toward the bedroom to give his wife the bad news: "This could not have happened in America, despite her many faults."

"Yaabo, wake up. There is a military takeover of the Mpata government, and I am one of the persons expected to report at the police station for my own safety," Ifok said.

"Oh my God!" Yaabo exclaimed. "What are we going to do? So there is finally a military coup in this country. I thought our country was different from other African countries," she said.

"I feel safe here and I am not going to any police station for my own safety," Ifok said.

"What are you going to do?" Yaabo asked, not expecting an answer.

After a short pause, Yaabo suggested that Ifok should go and hide in the house of a family friend who lived three blocks away, at least, for twenty-four hours before surrendering, if at all. They felt that within that time they would learn of the fate of officials who surrendered. Yaabo called the family friend who agreed with the plan. Before Ifok left for his refuge, he made a promise to his wife: "We will go and settle in America as soon as this nonsense is over," he said.

"We will talk about that later. Let us think of your safety first," Yaabo said. Ifok, dressed like an old woman and with a cane, walked to the family friend's house.

The military music on the radio was interrupted at 10 AM with another announcement: "Good morning, countrymen. I am General Boko of the Armed Forces. The Armed Forces in cooperation with the Police Department have overthrown the corrupt civilian government of President Mpata. President Mpata is under house arrest. All Members of Parliament, Ministers and Secretaries of Ministries are to report at the nearest police station immediately for their own safety. The government is now being run by the Peoples' Council, which is made up of representatives of the Armed Forces and the Police Department. Membership of the council will be announced later in the day. The public is advised to remain calm and stay indoors. All acts of hooliganism and vandalism will be severely repressed."

At about 7.00 PM, ten soldiers in military jeeps arrived at Ifok's house. Eight of them, with weapons drawn, surrounded the house while two headed for the front door. Yaabo was on the phone with Ifok when she saw the two soldiers approach the door. She hung up immediately and walked toward the door.

"May I help you?" she asked.

"We are looking for Mr Ifok Hasnem," the leader of the group said.

"He left for the police station about two hours ago," Yaabo said.

"Anyway, who are you?" the leader asked Yaabo.

"I am Mr Hasnem's wife and an attorney with the Attorney General's Department," Yaabo responded.

"You are a very attractive woman," the leader said

"Thank you" Yaabo responded.

As soon as the soldiers left, Yaabo called Ifok at his hideout. Ifok expressed concern for her safety.

"I do not think you should be alone in that house. I do not trust these soldiers. Some of them may take the law into their own hands and terrorize law-abiding citizens. I will suggest that you call your mother tonight and go and live with her for sometime," Ifok said.

"I agree with you. I will do that as soon as I am through talking with you. Anyway, when are you going to the police?" Yaabo asked.

"By six in the morning," Ifok said. Before Yaabo could utter another word she saw about six soldiers walking toward her front door.

"I've got to go. The soldiers are back," she said to Ifok and hung up.

"Why did you lie to us?" the leader of the group asked Yaabo.

"We contacted all police stations and were told your husband had still not reported for his own safety. Where is he?" he asked.

"I only told you what he told me," Yaabo said.

"Start searching the house" the leader ordered his men.

Ifok called his house an hour later.

"May I speak with Mr Ifok Hasnem, please? He asked.

"He is not in at the moment," a male voice answered.

"May I speak to his wife? Ifok asked.

"She is also not in," the male voice answered

Ifok hung up but was very concerned about the safety of his wife. He decided to surrender immediately. He went to the nearest police station and was later transferred to the city jail like all the government officials. Yaabo's mother called her daughter's residence several times that night but there was no response. Because there was a curfew in effect from 6.00 PM to 6.00AM, she could not go to check on her that night. When she got there in the morning, the whole house was in disarray. She immediately reported to the police that her daughter was missing and that she suspected some soldiers had been at the house the previous night to arrest her son-in-law. Yaabo was never seen alive again. Two weeks later, her body was found buried in a shallow grave on the outskirts of the city. Members of a boys scout troop on a camping trip smelled a foul odor and saw the toes of a human being protruding from the ground near where they had set up their tent. The scoutmaster notified the police who exhumed the body and sent it to the government hospital for an autopsy. That concluded that Yaabo had been raped before being strangled to death.

Ifok felt very guilty about Yaabo's death.

"Maybe if I had reported at the nearest police station earlier, the rascals would not have had to come to my house to look for me," he told Yaabo's mother when she visited him in the city jail and told him of his wife's death.

"Well, there is nothing we can do now but hope that the soldiers responsible for this crime are arrested and punished," Yaabo's mother said.

"The brutes hardly punish their own kind. They raped my dear wife before killing her," Ifok said, tears running down his cheeks.

"The house is locked up now. Would you like me to ask your cousin, Apach, to go and live there till your release?" Yaabo's mother asked.

"Do whatever you think is appropriate. I am confused right now and cannot think straight," Ifok said.

The Military Police took over the investigation of Yaabo's death and within two weeks the six soldiers involved in this heinous crime had been arrested. They had not been authorized to kill anyone, not even Ifok. They had been drinking before they were ordered to go and arrest Ifok, and they took the law into their own hands when they found Yaabo alone in the house. On the orders of the Peoples' Council, these soldiers were court-martialed and executed by firing squad.

APPEARANCE AT
COMMISION OF
INQUIRY

All the detained politicians were scheduled to appear before the Assets Probe Commission for questioning. They were expected to produce documents pertaining to all properties owned and bank accounts.

"Briefly tell the commission all the properties and bank accounts you own in this country and abroad. Perjury carries a minimum of five years in prison with hard labor," the Chairman of the Commission told Ifok.

"I own one building, the one I live in, and have three bank accounts, all in this country. I do not have more than $12,000 in these accounts," Ifok said.

"Quaterly deductions of $500 are made from your account at Barclays Bank and sent to someone named Gama. Who is Gama, and what are the payments for? A member of the commission asked.

"Gama is my ex-wife and the payments have been for support of our son," Ifok replied.'How come a person of your standing has only $12,000 in his bank accounts?" another member of the commission asked.

"My job is my main source of income and I have a wife and a teen-aged son to support" Ifok replied.

"How many cars do you own? The chairman asked.

"One. It is a taxi which I purchased before I accepted my initial position," Ifok replied.

"You are telling this commission that you own only a house and a taxi and no more. You do not have hidden assets, do you? The chairman asked.

"No" Ifok answered.

Ifok's appearance before the Commission of Inquiry was followed by deep reflection and examination of his life and consideration of steps for moving on. His parents had died the previous year of old age, six months apart; he had not been able to establish a proper rapport with his son who had accepted his step-father as his father, and had become an adult and doing his own thing; and his wife had been killed during the military coup. The thought of returning to America scared the hell out of him but it was a very viable option.

The military coup was followed by the establishment of a new government and the automatic firing of the senior officials of the previous regime. If Ifok did not take immediate steps after his release from jail, his only source of income would be the proceeds from his one-cab business. He would also have to vacate his government bungalow and return to his parent's house.

CHAPTER 10

Back In The U.S.A

Ifok's assets were defrozen by the commission and he was released from jail. He was warned to not leave the country without permission from the Peoples' Council, since he could be called upon later in connection with the activities of his ministry. Immediately after his release, Ifok contacted the American Embassy which confirmed his status as a permanent resident of the United States. Within a few months, he was back in Chicago, Illinois, where he obtained employment as a night security guard while looking for a government job during the day. After working in such capacity for 9 months without obtaining his desired job, he moved to Houston, Texas. He met and married Effie, an African with training as a medical assistant, who was about fifteen years younger than he, and had been in the United States for less than 5 years.

Ifok's first job in Houston was as a pizza delivery driver. With his hair eighty percent gray and getting thinner, he was a standout among the drivers who were mainly students living at home. He got good tips and always came home with some pizza. This job was in the evening and that enabled him to apply for professional positions during the day. In about 6 months, he obtained employment at the main office of Peakload Services, a temporary employment agency. He cleaned the office building from 5 to 11 PM, Monday through Friday, and did the yard work of the facility for 4 hours on Saturdays.

After about 2 years on the job, Ifok had the opportunity to apply for a better position in that agency but he did not. The position that became open was that of mailroom clerk. The guy holding the position was fired for tardiness and absenteeism, and the manager advised Ifok to apply for it.

"I checked your record yesterday, and you are qualified for the mailroom clerk position," the manager stated. Ifok had stated on his application that he was a high school graduate and part-time student at a local community college.

"You appear to be quite educated and speak the language well. Let me know by the end of the week if you will be interested in the position," the manager continued.

Ifok notified her the next day that he was not interested in the position because working a 9 to 5 job would interfere with his education.

After months of applying for State of Texas positions – about 50—requiring a bachelor's degree with no more than 2 years of experience, a friend advised Ifok to file a formal complaint with the EEOC (Equal Employment

Opportunity Commission). For this complaint, Ifok selected positions requiring bachelor's degrees with no experience, or master's degrees. The State of Texas was ordered to provide the applications of those hired for the positions, and examination of those documents indicated Ifok was more qualified than most of those hired. The EEOC then gave Ifok the right to sue the State of Texas for employment discrimination.

Getting a good lawyer to file an employment discrimination lawsuit against the State of Texas was not easy. Ifok wanted a lawyer on a contingency basis, whereby he or she would take a percentage, usually 33.3 percent, of any award. After months of trying without success to find such an attorney, Ifok decided to file the lawsuit pro se. He still needed a good attorney to prepare the original complaint. He was charged $500 for that service, and just before filing the lawsuit at the United States District Court, he was introduced to a young lawyer who agreed to take the case on a contingency basis.

Ifok's lawyer filed the lawsuit and then contacted the Attorney General's Department which would be representing the three State agencies cited in the complaint. After about a month, Ifok's attorney informed him that she and the Assistant State Attorney handling the case had agreed to the following: the case would be handled by the Magistrate Court and not the District Court; both parties would try to resolve the issue through arbitration; and if that failed then by the Magistrate Court. Ifok was very excited at the prospect for arbitration of this issue; he was sure he would get a State job.

The arbitration was held at the conference room of a law firm in Downtown Houston. The arbitrator, a prominent lawyer who later became a judge introduced himself and stated the purpose of the meeting. The State of Texas was represented by the Assistant Attorney General and 6 officials (2 from the State capital of Austin and 4 from Houston). Of course, Ifok and his attorney were also present. Ifok's attorney made a nice presentation based on the facts of the case, followed by Ifok who gave a narration of the number of positions he had applied for and his qualifications; for resolution, Ifok proposed a year's salary and a job offer. The Assistant Attorney General offered Ifok and his lawyer $5,000 but made no job offer, claiming all the positions cited by Ifok were filled by equally qualified applicants. Ifok rejected the offer, and in a private discussion with his attorney he rejected her suggestion to accept the offer. Later, the case was dismissed with prejudice by the Magistrate, meaning Ifok could re-file it at a future date. The case with the State of Texas lasted almost 3 years. After the verdict, Ifok continued working as a janitor/yard man while still looking for other employment during the regular work week.

The Welfare-To-Work Act of 1997 resulted in the privatization of some governmental services. An American friend who used to work for the Texas Department of Human Services had the functions of his division transferred to Houston Works, a non-profit employment services agency. This guy talked to his manager, Mr Trane, about Ifok and his background. Mr Trane hired Ifok as a workforce development specialist in the non-custodial parent program. Ifok's responsibilities included the following: identification of non-custodial parents eligible for services, which consisted mainly of case management and job development activities. He received referrals from the courts and the attorney-general's department, and visited local jails to inform inmates about to be released about the availability of the non-custodial parent program.

Many participants in the non-custodial parent program had had some interaction with law enforcement or social service departments or agencies—incarceration, probation, parole, substance abuse etc.—in the past. They were mainly men but there were a few women who were eligible. After Ifok received lists of eligible applicants from the courts and the Attorney General's Department every month, he sent letters of invitation to them. Only about 30 percent of these persons showed up at his office as instructed. The remaining 70 percent he had to go to their last addresses of record to look for them, and that proved to be the hardest part of his job.

It appeared eligible parents were not interested in the program because the courts had a system in place to collect past due child support and payment for public support for their children, as soon as they obtained suitable employment. These addresses were usually in the poorest neighborhoods with high crime rates, and they reminded Ifok of the public housing projects in Chicago, Illinois. On a number of occasions he drove to some addresses but could not get out of his car because of fear for his safety. Ifok stayed on that job for a total of 2 years till he was hired by the Texas Department of Assistive and Rehabilitative Services (DARS) as a vocational rehabilitation counselor.

VOCATIONAL
REHABILITATION
COUNSELOR

Ifok had applied for the vocational rehabilitation counselor position at four field offices of DARS in the past but was never interviewed, even though he was highly qualified: a masters degree and about 5 years experience in eligibility determination, preparation of service plans, job placement etc. The manager who interviewed Ifok was himself an immigrant, having moved to this country twenty-five years ago just like Ifok. Both he and Ifok had some other things in common—they were originally from countries formerly colonized by the British, and were about the same age. The interview went very well and Ifok was hired for the position. The rules of DARS required new vocational rehabilitation counselors without a masters in that field to complete a minimum of 18 graduate level credits, at the agency's expense, in 7 years or lose their jobs. Ifok met this requirement in two years and was designated as a QVRC (Qualified Vocational Rehabilitation Counselor).

Ifok liked this job, the best he had had in terms of renumeration. His responsibilities included provision of rehabilitation services for persons with disabilities to enhance their employment prospects. The process involved profile development, eligibility determination, and preparation of plans for employment based on informed client choice. Ifok served as liaison to some agency vendors and helped resolve programmatic issues.

The vocational rehabilitation program had a referral system in place which allowed service providers - training institutions, half-way houses, social service agencies etc.—to refer clients to DARS for services.

These providers were often invited to staff meetings to inform staff about their programs. According to the rules, persons on disability benefits were presumed eligible for services, unless determined otherwise. As a result of the above, there were some situations where some clients were declared eligible for services even though they did not meet the major criterion of "capability of an employment outcome."

Counselors had almost complete control of their caseloads. They were allocated funds each year which they were to use to put a specified number of persons with disabilities to work, and that was not easy. The agency appeared to be more interested in employment outcomes and these were used as a major criterion in evaluation of counselors. Managers exercised limited control over counselors' accounts and caseload actions. One could sense instances of cronyism and favoritism when reading cases. On a number of occasions when counselors were found to have accepted kickbacks or bribes, or provided illicit outcome numbers, such counselors faced severe punishment, including termination.

One day, on a visit to a school with a DARS contract, Ifok was approached by a senior official of that institution.

"Do you want to make some money," the official asked Ifok.

"What do you mean by that," Ifok asked, not understanding what the official was talking about.

"I have 5 students needing services from DARS. If you can make them eligible and pay for their training here, I will give you $500, that is $100 for each student," the official continued.

Ifok was surprised by the boldness of the school official. He was visibly shaken by the proposal.

"Sir, as an official of the State of Texas I am paid well, and I do not need a kickback to supplement my income. I traveled a bumpy, long and winding road to get to where I am now, and frankly, I consider your request an insult," Ifok said. "And, do I look like someone on the take?" he asked the official.

"No, I thought you were someone I could work with," the official said.

"Please, please, please, never talk to me like that again," Ifok concluded.

Ifok did not discuss this issue with his supervisor, since attempts by vendors to influence counselors were well-known within the agency. Ifok worked for the department for a total of eleven years, the last five of which he was assigned the additional responsibilities of back-up manager of his office. An honorary position, it involved being in charge of the office in the absence of the manager, and handling programmatic and staff issues as they arose. He retired at age 65.

Ifok and Effie now have 3 sons, two of whom are in college. The family visited Africa when the children were younger. The children have no plans to live in Africa, neither does Ifok. Effie continues to dream about returning to Africa some day, just like Ifok did when he was younger.

www.ingramcontent.com/pod-product-compliance
Lightning Source LLC
Chambersburg PA
CBHW020428290526
45785CB00002B/756